THE FRUGAL
COLONIAL HOUSEWIFE

THE
FRUGAL HOUSEWIFE
OR
Complete Woman Cook.

WHEREIN

The Art of Dressing all Sorts of Viands
with Cleanliness, Decency, and Elegance,

Is explained in

Five Hundred approved RECEIPTS, in

Roasting,	Pasties,
Boiling,	Pies,
Frying,	Tarts,
Broiling,	Cakes,
Gravies,	Puddings,
Sauces,	Syllabubs,
Stews,	Creams,
Hashes,	Flummery,
Soups,	Jellies,
Fricassees,	Giams, and
Ragoos,	Custards.

Together with the BEST METHODS of

Potting,	Drying,
Collaring,	Candying,
Preserving,	Pickling,

And making of ENGLISH WINES.

To which are prefixed,

Various BILLS OF FARE,

For DINNERS and SUPPERS in every Month of the Year;
and a copious INDEX to the whole.

By SUSANNAH CARTER,
Of CLERKENWELL,

LONDON.

Printed for F. NEWBERY, at the Corner of St. Paul's
Church-Yard

BOSTON:

Re-Printed and Sold by EDES and GILL, in Queenstreet.

Copy of the original title page.

THE FRUGAL COLONIAL HOUSEWIFE

A Cook's Book

wherein
The Art of Dressing all Sorts
of Viands with Cleanliness, Decency,
and Elegance is explained

by Susannah Carter

edited and illustrated by
Jean McKibbin

DOLPHIN BOOKS
Doubleday & Company, Inc.
GARDEN CITY, NEW YORK
1976

The title of the original book which, for the most part, is reproduced here as it was written by Susannah Carter was *The Frugal Colonial Housewife or Complete Woman Cook*, published in 1772. The text material from Susannah Carter's original book retains her spellings but has been reset for the Dolphin edition. The Introduction to this edition was not part of the original text but has been added here as an aid for the reader to better capture the flavor of the original.

Wall sconce.

Library of Congress Cataloging in Publication Data

Carter, Susannah.
    The frugal colonial housewife.

    First published in 1772 under title: The frugal housewife.
    1. Cookery—Early works to 1800. I. Title.
TX703.C37 1976   641.5
        ISBN 0-385-11259-9
Library of Congress Catalog Card Number 75–21249

Dolphin Edition: 1976

Contents

Contents

The cleaned and combed wool was spun into yarn on a wheel such as this. A housewife might walk as much as twenty miles a day, half of it backward, as she fed the wool, kept the big wheel turning and drew out the yarn.

Introduction

Copy of a lantern much like the one carried by Paul Revere.

The Frugal Housewife or Complete Woman Cook by Susannah Carter was the only cookbook printed in this country between 1742 and 1796, a period that included both the late Colonial and the early years of these United States. In this book we have reset the type from Miss Carter's book for readability and have added a generous serving of illustrations and captions, as well as a glossary to clarify the meaning of words no longer in common usage. The original title page and the two plates engraved by Paul Revere are reproduced here exactly as they were in 1772 when the book was first published. Language and spelling are left as they were written two hundred years ago.

Where history books abound with battles and political maneuvering *The Frugal Housewife* shows the warm earthiness of home and hearth, family and friends, food and drink in the years when our forefathers established this nation.

Most of us learned our American history in stuffy grammar school classrooms. We have vague recollections of dates that colonies were settled and the succession of the Presidents. Tucked in here and there are more dates for wars and rebellions plus, on rare occasions, the name of a man who helped shape the growth of America. Few of us have any real understanding of the people themselves.

The total population in 1776 was a bare two and a half million. This is considerably less than are concentrated today in the greater Boston area. Yet the new Americans of two hundred years ago were spread out over what is today thirteen states. Ninety-five per cent of them were farmers. The 100,000 or so who lived in the cities and villages along the northern coast and rivers were generally small-craftsmen who sold goods or made by hand the shoes or shovels or harness required by town and country folk alike.

The constant quarreling between the European nations who were struggling for possession of the New World led to a general air of uncertainty as to the future. To the south, at St. Augustine, Florida, was the Spanish settlement but their interest was directed more toward Central and South America. Sweden's forts along the Delaware River had been taken by the Dutch in 1655, but they in turn had lost the New Netherland colony to the English in 1664. From 1689 to 1763 the French and English fought intermittently for the rich fur trade and the Atlantic fisheries.

A brick oven built into the fireplace.

Eventually France gave up all North American territory except two small islands off the coast of Canada.

To pay the costs of these wars with France, England had taxed the colonists heavily. She had also interfered with Colonial trade and self-government. Finally, in 1775, the colonists united to fight the Revolutionary War. But it was not until 1783 that England signed the treaty of peace and acknowledged the independence of the colonies.

This is the backdrop for the birth of our country. The land was barely settled. Indians roamed over most of it. The West was undiscovered. And life was simple if we take "simple" to mean that conveniences were few and even the necessities were strictly homemade.

The sounds of the country tell us much about how life was lived—the ring of falling axes, the tread of heavy boots, shouts of peddlers and town criers, the clatter of spinning wheels and the click of looms, the thump and splash of churns, and the distant booming of the fulling mills.

The smells of early America tell us more—fresh baked bread and beans, pickling spices in hot vinegar, curing hams hanging in the smokehouse and the roast turning slowly on the spit before the fire, new-mown hay drying in the meadow, and everywhere the smell of smoke and burning wood.

The original settlers were British men and women. From Massachusetts Bay to Georgia the villages were groups of good and sturdy men of sound common sense. The one interruption in the long line of British colonies was Dutch Nieuw Amsterdam. Even in the following early waves of migration, the people were predominantly British. The Quakers of Pennsylvania were Welsh, and the Scotch-Irish from the Scottish Lowlands and northern England had lived in Ulster for years before making the move across the Atlantic.

The clipper ship, a link not only between America and Europe, but also the most common means of transportation between the colonies themselves.

A wooden latch with the string pushed out through a small hole in the door. An early sign of welcome, for the door could then be opened from without. Origin of the expression, "The string is out."

As time passed the immigrants came in an ever increasing flood. Among them new names and nationalities appeared—the Germans from the Rhine, Huguenots from France, and the Swiss. Still the colonies remained predominantly British as the newcomers absorbed the habits and the outlook as well as the language. They cleared the land and planted. They set up their local governments and businesses. They traded among themselves and with England. And everywhere they went they built their homes.

History books offer descriptions of the huge and stately mansions—from Wynnstay, the home of Thomas Wynn, near Philadelphia, to the mansions of the southern plantations. But these homes, as beautiful as they were, were the exception. Most homes in early America were only one large room. As families grew, additional lean-to rooms were added, but the one room, the common room, was the heart of the house.

Much more than the cooking and eating of meals took place in the common room. The fireplace dominated, of course, with all the assorted tools and utensils used in preparing the meals standing nearby or hanging from pegs in the wall. As this was frequently the only "fire room" in the house, it was also the room where the family lived. A high bed filled one corner of the room with a trundle bed pushed beneath it when it was not in use. There were stools and chairs to sit upon, a chest or sometimes a chest of drawers, shelves with wooden plates and trenchers and the pewter on display. There was a water pail and a wash bench, barrels for salt meat and fish, corn meal and flour, molasses, cider and beer, and kegs to store gunpowder and rum. A flintlock rifle or two hung from pegs, as did the extra clothing, for there were no closets. In one corner stood the spinning wheel for wool or flax, a reel for yarn, and sometimes even a loom. Certainly it was crowded, but not so much that one more item couldn't be added. The bench before the fireplace was an important part of the settler's life. Here he and his wife might sit to warm themselves when their long day's work was finished. The problem was that the great fireplaces created a very cold draft on their backs while they sought to warm themselves. The settler solved the problem by adding a high wooden back to the bench with plain board wings at either end. As a table was needed only at mealtime, and as space was ever a problem in the common room, the early settler went one step further with the settle bench. By putting the back on pivots where it joined the arms, it could be tipped forward to become a broad table when needed.

As houses grew, another room might be added as a "cooking room," a kitchen, with its own fireplace which was at least eight and often as much as ten feet wide.

One corner of the common room, the heart of the house. The settle bench, a place to sit at the end of the day, its high back and wings to protect against the cold drafts. In time of need the hinged back could tip forward and become a table, while the space below held a variety of small possessions.

Here the curious contrivances of long-handled waffle irons, bread toasters and gridirons, heavy pots hanging on cranes built into the fireplace wall, and roasting ovens that stood before the fire give an insight to the singed eyebrows, perspiring foreheads and the stamina that characterized the homemaker in those early days.

The most common method of cooking was boiling. Pots and kettles hung by pothooks on lugpoles in the fireplace or by trammels from cranes. Lugpoles were unhandy for the heavy pots had to be lifted in and out over the fire. Besides, as they were usually a wooden pole, they tended to burn through, and the whole dinner might well end up in the ashes. The crane was a great improvement. With it the pot could be swung out to season or taste or to test if the meat was "enough." Boiling pots required little attention. So long as the water didn't waste away completely or the fire die down, dinner went right on cooking.

Roasting was another method of cooking, this before the open hearth. A spit was thrust through the meat and supported by two forked uprights. The roasting meat was turned constantly either by a small boy or a device attached to chains that fitted over cogged wheels similar to the clockworks. A pan beneath caught the drippings for sauce or gravy. The difficulty with roasting was that the meat tended to cool off on the side toward the room just about as fast as it heated on the side toward the fire. This was essentially the same problem that the settler and his wife had had when they were warming themselves on the old bench. For both problems they developed similar solutions. Thus the roasting oven evolved. It consisted of a

The foot warmer was a small metal box with a wooden frame that could be filled with hot coals and carried to church or meeting place when days were cold and there was no heating.

spit, supports, and the pan beneath, plus a hood and a back that provided protection from the cool drafts in the room. At the same time it reflected the heat from the fire to the back of the roast as it turned on the spit. There was a hinged lid in the hood to provide access to the meat for basting. Broiling was akin to roasting. Smaller pieces of meat were placed on a gridiron and cooked over the glowing coals.

Baking was done in a closed receptacle or in an oven rather than before the open fire. Cast-iron pots with heavy lids were set into the hot ashes. An upright rim on the lid permitted coals to be heaped on the top too. The next development was the brick oven, which was a good-sized hole in the chimney with its own small flue opening into the main one. An iron door closed the front opening. A hot fire was built in the oven. When the bricks were well heated, the wood and ashes were swept out, the flue closed, and the food put in. Then the door was tightly closed until the baking was done, a length of time determined by experience alone. Most of the "roasted" meat today is really baked.

Frying in the long-handled frying pan was the final method of cooking. This was the hardest to learn for the pan had to be shaken frequently not only to keep the contents from burning but also to mix in added ingredients and seasonings.

The lady of the house milked and churned, sowed and reaped her vegetable garden, carded and spun the wool, and wove the woolen cloth from which she then sewed the family's clothes. She gathered herbs and was, in many cases, the family

Roasting was done on a spit before the open fire. Meat, turning on the spit, cooled on the side away from the fire, making cooking difficult. The addition of a hood and back prevented this from happening. A pan beneath caught the drippings, and the hinged back permitted access for basting and testing.

physician. Her dress was simple, long-skirted, made of wool or a coarse, sturdy fabric with linen warp and woolen filling known as "linsey-woolsey." Her good man wore "small clothes," breeches, tied just below his knee and a long shirt wrapped about him and tied closed with a belt. In the folds of his belt he carried a knife, sometimes a hatchet, and frequently a piece of dried beef or venison "jerky" that would be his meal away from home. Both wore sturdy shoes, handmade in the village and repaired at home. As they were not mated right and left, they had to be switched daily to keep the wear even.

The busy housewife might make her own soap and candles, plant and reap and spin and sew during the hours she wasn't watching her fire and the kettles and pots of food, but she had help from many hands. During the summer and fall months when roads were passable the itinerant workers made their way through the country. They took their pay in whatever surplus materials the settler had.

The man who made shoes was known as a "cordwainer." If he also repaired shoes he was called a "cat whipper."

The housewife washed and carded the wool and cleaned the flax. From them both she spun yarn throughout the year. But if she had a large family and needed help in weaving, the traveling weaver was there. The tailor followed behind the weaver to make coats and breeches and capes.

The housewife made candles by repeatedly dipping wicks into tallow or in tin molds that made six to a dozen at once, but the traveling "chandler" brought his own big molds that made six dozen at a time. The "tinker" was a summer visitor too, but stayed only a day or two to repair dippers and basins.

The nearest town had tradesmen to supply other needs. Barbers and wigmakers were adept at pulling teeth and letting blood, an operation believed to relieve many illnesses. The apothecary not only mixed medicines, but also prescribed them and visited the sick. (The United States had no pharmacopoeia until 1820, no college of pharmacy until 1841, and no pharmaceutical code of ethics until 1856).

There were bakers, hatters, tobacconists, eyeglass sellers, and cutlers. Some blacksmiths made to order the many iron items used for cooking from pothooks to rotatable grills. Others shoed animals or specialized in the iron work for wagons and carriages. The locksmith was also a member of the blacksmith trade. Then there was the whitesmith who was later known as the tinsmith, and men who worked in copper, pewter, and silver. Other shops might include a cabinetmaker, printer, coachmaker, weaver, potter, or cooper, a man who made barrels.

In the smaller villages a school of sorts was conducted by a "dame," often a widow, who taught alphabet and catechism and sometimes reading and writing. Larger towns had grammar schools where reading, writing, arithmetic, and religion were taught. The few colleges of this period concentrated on the study of the classics.

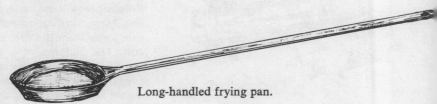

Long-handled frying pan.

The leaves of the flax plant were soaked and beaten until only the long, strong fibers remained. These were spun on a small wheel to make fine linen thread.

The vast majority of the population was rural and most of them could not read or write. There was little need for cookbooks and very few were printed. In Williamsburg in 1742 a reprint of an English cookbook was printed. It was *The Compleat Housewife or Accomplish'd Gentlewoman's Companion* by E. (Elizabeth or Eliza) Smith. During the following fifty long years—from 1742 until 1792—there was only one cookbook printed in this country. This was *The Frugal Housewife or Complete Woman Cook* by Susannah Carter. In 1772 it was printed and sold by Eads and Gill in Queenstreet, Boston. The date of publication has been fixed by an advertisement in the Boston *Gazette* for Monday, March 2, 1772. There was possibly a reprint of this book in 1774, but no copies are now known to exist. It was a long-lived title though, for it appeared again in 1792, printed for Berry and Rogers, No. 35 Hanover Square, New York. Other editions followed— 1795—Berry and Rogers, New York; 1796, James Carey, Philadelphia; 1802, Mathew Carey, Philadelphia; and 1803 G. and R. Waite, New York.

And so, as it was the only cookbook printed in America during the very formative years of pre- and post-Revolutionary times, we feel that it is a major part of our history that has been neglected and unrecognized. History books fill their pages with peace, wars, rebellions and uprisings, with new governments and new "colonies-*cum*-states." Now we have turned these pages back to look for what is missing and we have found the fascinating story of how man filled his belly before going to war or making peace.

Sturdy shoes, handmade by the "cordwainer" in the village were not mated right and left. They had to be switched daily to keep the wear even.

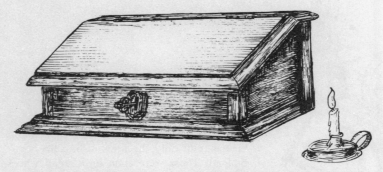

A small, hinged-top desk took up little room. It could be locked and carried from place to place yet provide a surface on which to write when needed.

You will soon discover as you read this book that Miss Carter's "receipts" for cooking were very much in the English manner. There is no mention of many of the native American foods such as beans, corn, squash, cranberries, and pumpkin, all of which were in common use. She does, however, discuss turkey, potatoes, and turtle which, along with tobacco, had made their way to England at a very early date. They had been assimilated into the English cuisine and returned to these shores as accepted English dishes. This book was probably prepared for and used by the wealthy segment of the population who lived in an elegant manner that mirrored English life. They often had French or English cooks in their kitchens. A good indication that this was the case is the lavish use of lemons and oranges with the meats and fish. Citrus fruits were available on a limited basis in the seaport cities where sailing ships docked from Spain. What citrus was available was much too expensive for most people.

Modern American cuisine is a blending of the memories of the French, Dutch, Spanish, Scotch-Irish, and Germans. None the less, the strongest influence on the development of our present cuisine was the English. Hence, the importance of the book that follows. For not only was it *the* cookbook at the time of our American Revolution; but more importantly it reveals the basic elements of our American cooking heritage.

THE FRUGAL
COLONIAL HOUSEWIFE

A Hare or Rabbit trussed for Roasting

A Hare or Rabbit for Roasting or Boiling

A Goose

Breast   Ducks   Back

Copy of a plate engraved by Paul Revere for the original book.

A BILL of FARE
for Every Month in the Year

In JANUARY

Dinner

Beef Soup, made with brisket of beef; and the beef served up in the dish. *Turkey* and *Chine roasted,* with gravy and onion sauce; minced pies.

Or,

A *chine of beef* boiled and carrots and savoys, with melted butter, *hare* and *fowls* roasted, with rich gravy; *tarts.*

Or,

Vermicelli soup, fore quarter of lamb and sallad in season; *fresh salmon,* a sufficient quantity boiled, with smelts fried, and lobster sauce; *minced pies.*

Supper

Chicken fricassees; *wild ducks* with rich gravy sauce; piece of *sturgeon* or brawn, and *minced pies.*

Or,

A *hare,* with pudding in its belly, and strong gravy and claret sauce; *hen turkey* boiled and oyster sauce, and onion sauce; *brawn,* and *minced pies.*

In FEBRUARY

Dinner

Chine or saddle of mutton roasted, with pickles; *calve's head* boiled and grilled, garnished with boiled slices of bacon, and with brains mashed with parsley and butter, salt, pepper, and a little vinegar: the tongue slit and laid upon the brains; a *boiled pudding.*

Or,
Ham and *fowls* roasted, with gravy sauce; *leg of lamb* boiled, with spinach.
Or,
A piece of *fresh salmon,* with lobster sauce, and garnished with fried *smelts,* or *flounders; chickens* roasted and asparagus, with gravy and plain butter.

Supper

Scotch collops, ducklings, with rich gravy; *minced pies.*
Or,
Fried *soles* with shrimp sauce; fore quarter of lamb roasted, with mint sauce; dish of *tarts* and *custards*.

Dill   Anise   Fennel

In MARCH

Dinner

Roast beef, and horse-radish to garnish the dish; *salt-fish* with egg sauce, and potatoes or parsnips, with melted butter; *pease soup.*
Or,
Ham, and *fowls* roasted; *marrow pudding.*
Or,
Leg of *Mutton* boiled, with turnips and caper sauce; *Cod* boiled with oyster sauce and garnished with horse-radish; *A bread pudding.*

Supper

Scollops or *fried oysters; leg of lamb,* with spinach; *tarts* and *fruit.*
Or,
Fricassee of coxcombs, lambstones, and sweetbreads; *pigeon pie* and *marrow pudding.*

In APRIL

Dinner

Ham and *chicken* roasted, with gravy sauce; a piece of boiled *beef,* and carrots and greens.

Or,

A roasted *shoulder* of *veal* stuff'd, and melted butter; a *leg* of *pork* boiled and pease pudding.

Or,

A dish of fish, (as in season) *roast beef* garnished with horse-radish and *plumb pudding.*

Supper

Fricassee of lambstones and sweetbreads, or sucking rabbits, roasted *pigeons* and asparagus.

Or,

Boiled *fowls* and *bacon,* or pickled *pork,* with greens and butter melted; a baked *plumb pudding* or *tarts.*

In MAY

Dinner

Beef soup, with herbs well boiled, *fillet of veal* well stuffed and roasted; a *ham* boiled.

Or,

Rump of beef salted and boiled, with a summer cabbage; *fresh salmon* boiled, and fried smelts to garnish the dish, with lobster or shrimp sauce.

Or,

Saddle of mutton roasted, with a spring sallad, and a dish of *fish.*

Supper

Ducklings roasted, with gravy sauce; *Scotch collops* with mushrooms, &c., *tarts.*

Or,

Green goose, with gravy sauce; *collared eels,* and *tarts.*

In JUNE

Dinner

Leg of grass lamb boiled, with capers, carrots, and turnips, *shoulder or neck of venison* roasted, with rich gravy and claret sauce; *marrow pudding.*

Or,

Saddle of grass lamb roasted, with mint sauce and turnips; *turbot* boiled, with shrimp and anchovy sauce; a *quaking pudding.*

Or,

A haunch of venison roasted, with rich gravy and claret sauce; *tarts.*

Supper

Fricassee of young rabbits, roast *fowls* and gravy sauce; *gooseberry tarts.*

Or,

Makarel boiled, with plain butter and makarel herbs; *leg of lamb* boiled and spinach.

In JULY

Dinner

Green Goose, with gravy sauce; *neck of veal* boiled with *bacon* and greens.

Or,

Mackarel boiled, with melted butter and herbs; *fore quarter of lamb,* with sallad of fresh lettuce &c.

Supper

Chickens roasted, with gravy or egg sauce; *lobsters* or *prawns; green pease.*

Or,

Stewed *carp; ducklings,* with gravy sauce; *beans.*

In AUGUST

Dinner

Ham, and *fowls* roasted, with gravy sauce; *beans.*

Or,

Neck of *venison,* with gravy and claret sauce; *fresh salmon,* with lobster sauce; *apple pie,* hot and buttered.

Or,

Beef a-la-mode; green pease; haddock boiled, and fried *soles* or *flounders* to garnish the dish.

Supper

White *fricassee of chickens; green pease; ducks* roasted, with gravy sauce.

Or,

Chickens or *pigeons* roasted, with *asparagus; artichokes,* with melted butter.

Or,

Neck of venison, with gravy and claret sauce; *fresh salmon,* with lobster sauce; *apple pie,* hot and buttered.

Or,

Beef a-la-mode; green pease; haddock boiled, and fried *soles* or *flounders* to garnish the dish.

Supper

White *fricassee of chickens; green pease; ducks* roasted, with gravy sauce.
Or,
Chickens or *pigeons* roasted, with *asparagus; artichokes,* with melted butter.

In SEPTEMBER

Dinner

Green Pease soup; breast of veal roasted; boiled plain pudding.
Or,
Leg of lamb boiled, with turnips, spinach, and caper sauce; *goose* roasted, with gravy, mustard and apple sauce; and *pigeon pie.*

Supper

Boiled *pullets,* with oyster sauce, green beans and bacon; dish of fried *soles.*
Or,
A grouse, with gravy sauce; *wild ducks* with gravy sauce and onion sauce; *apple pie.*

In OCTOBER

Dinner

Cod's head, with shrimp and oyster sauce; *knuckle of veal* and bacon, and greens.

Or,

Leg of mutton boiled, with turnips and caper sauce; *Scotch Collops;* fresh *salmon* boiled, with shrimp and anchovy sauce.
Or,
Calf's head dressed turtle fashion; *roast beef,* with horse-radish; *beef* soup.

Supper

Wild ducks, with gravy sauce, scalloped oysters; *minced* pies.
Or,
Fried smelts, with anchovy sauce; boiled *fowl,* with oyster sauce; *minced pies* or *tarts.*

Calf's head.

In NOVEMBER

Dinner

A roasted *goose* with gravy, and apple sauce, and mustard; *cod's head*, with oyster sauce; minced pies.

Or,

Roast *tongue* and *udder;* roast *fowls,* and *pigeon pie.*

Supper

Stewed *carp, calf's head* hashed; *minced pies.*

In DECEMBER

Dinner

Ham, and *fowls* roasted, with greens and gravy sauce; *gravy soup, fresh salmon,* garnished with whiting or trout fried, and with anchovy sauce.

Or,

Cod's head, with shrimp and oyster sauce; roast *beef,* garnished with horse-radish, and *plumb pudding* boiled.

Or,

Roast *beef,* with horse-radish; marrow pudding, and Scotch collops.

Supper

Brawns; pullets boiled and oyster sauce: and *minced pies.*

Or,

Broil'd chickens with mushrooms; a hare or wild rabbit with rich gravy sauce, *minced pies.*

Natural gas was discovered in this country in 1775, when a pioneer found "burning springs" in what is now West Virginia. George Washington claimed the land two years later. But it was thirty years before the first use of gas was made for lighting.

A Turkey for Roasting

A Turkey or Fowl for Boiling

A Chicken or Fowl for Roasting

A Pheasant or Patridge

Woodcock or Snipe

A Pigeon

Copy of a plate engraved by Paul Revere for the original book.

Chap. I

Of Roasting

General Rules to Be Observed in Roasting

Your fire must be made in proportion to the piece you are to dress; that is, if it be a little or thin piece, make a small brisk fire that it may be done quick and nice, but if a large joint, observe to lay a good fire to *cake,* and let it be always clear at the bottom. Allowing a quarter of an hour for every pound of meat at a ready fire your expectations will hardly ever fail from a surloin of beef to a small joint; nevertheless, I shall mention some few observations as to beef, mutton, lamb, veal, pork &c.

Ducks roasting on a spit.

Butcher's Meat

To Roast Beef

If it be a surloin or chump, butter a piece of writing paper, and fasten it to the back of your meat, with small skewers, and lay it down to a roasting fire, at a proper distance. As soon as your meat is warm, dust on some flour, and baste it with butter; then sprinkle some salt, and at times, baste with what drips from it.

About a quarter of an hour before you take it up, remove the paper, dust on a little flour, and baste with a piece of butter, that it may go to table with a good froth. Garnish your dish with scraped horse-radish, and serve it up with potatoes, broccoli, French beans, colliflower, horseradish or cellery.

To Roast Mutton

If a chine or saddle of mutton, let the skin be raised, and then skewered on again, this will prevent it from scorching, and make it eat mellow. A quarter of an hour before you take it up take off the skin, dust it with some flour and baste it with butter. Sprinkle on a little salt. As the chine, saddle, and leg are the largest joints they require a stronger fire than the shoulder, neck, or loin. Garnish with scrapped horse-radish; and serve it with potatoes, brocali, French beans, colliflower, water cresses, or horse-radish.

You may serve up a shoulder of mutton with onion sauce, if approved of.

To Roast Mutton Venison Fashion

Take a hind quarter of mutton, and cut the leg like a haunch; lay it in a pan with the back side of it down, pour a bottle of red wine over it, and let it lie twenty four hours; then spit it and baste it with the same liquor and butter all the time it is roasting at a good quick fire, and two hours and a half will do it. Have a little good gravy in a cup, and current jelly in another. A good fat neck of mutton eats finely done thus.

To Roast a Breast of Mutton with Forc'd Meat

A breast of mutton dressed thus is very good; the forced meat must be put under the skin at the end, and then the skin pinned down with horns: before you dredge it, wash it over with a bunch of feathers dipt in egg with lemon, and put good gravy in the dish.

A roasting oven.

A Shoulder or Leg of Mutton Stuffed

Stuff a leg of mutton with mutton suet, salt, pepper, nutmeg, and the yoke of eggs; then roast it. Stick it all over with cloves and when it is about half done, cut off some of the under side of the fleshy end in little bits, put those into a pipkin with a pint of oysters, liquor and all, a little salt and mace, and half a pint of hot water; stew them until half the liquor is wasted, then put in a piece of butter rolled in flour, shake all together and when the mutton is done enough, take it up; pour the sauce over it, and send it to the table.

To Roast a Tongue or Udder

Parboil it first, then roast it; stick eight or ten cloves about it, baste it with butter, and send it up with gravy and sweet sauce. An udder eats very well done the same way.

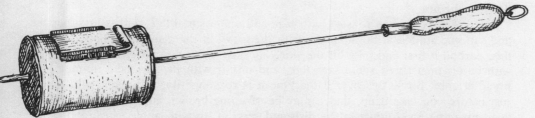

Coffee roaster. Coffee took the place of tea following the Boston Tea Party.

To Roast Lamb

Lay it down to a clear good fire, that will want little stirring; then baste it with butter, and dust on a little flour; baste it with what falls from it; and a little before you take it up, baste it again with butter, and sprinkle on a little salt and parsley shred fine. Send it up to table with a nice salad, mint sauce, green peas, french beans, or colliflower.

To Roast Veal

When you roast the loin, or fillet, paper the udder of the fillet, to preserve the fat, and the back of the loin, to preserve it from scorching; lay the meat at first some distance from the fire: that it may soak; baste it well with butter, then dust on a little flour. When it has soaked some time draw it nearer the fire: and a little before you take it up, baste it again. Most people chuse to stuff a fillet. The breast you must roast with the caul on, and the sweetbread skewered on the backside: when it is near enough, take off the caul, and baste it with butter. It is proper to have a toast nicely baked and laid in the dish with a loin of veal. Garnish with lemon.

The stuffing for a fillet of veal is made in the following manner; take about a pound of grated bread, half a pound of suet, some parsley shred fine, thyme, marjorum, or savory, which you like best, a little grated nutmeg, lemon peel, pepper and salt, and mix these well together with the whites and yolks of eggs.

To Roast Pork

Pork requires more doing than any other meat; and it is best to sprinkle it with a little salt the night before you use it, and hang it up: by that means it will take off the faint sickly taste.

When you roast a chine of pork, lay it down to a good fire, and at proper distance, that it may be well soaked.

A spare rib is to be roasted with a fire that is not too strong, but clear; when you lay it down, dust on some flour, and baste it with butter: a quarter of an hour before you take it up, shred some sage small; baste your pork; strew on the sage; dust on a little flour, and sprinkle a little salt before you take it up.

A loin must be cut on the skin in small streaks, and then basted; but put no flour on, which would make the skin blister; and see that it is jointed before you lay it down to the fire.

A leg of pork is often roasted with sage and onion shred fine, with a little pepper and salt and stuffed at the knuckle, with the gravy in the dish, but a better way is this, parboil it first and take off the skin; lay it down to a good clear fire. Baste it with butter then shred some sage fine, and mix it with pepper; take nutmeg and bread crumbs. Strew this over it the time it is roasting: Baste it again with butter just before you take it up, that it may be of a fine brown, and have a nice froth. Send up some good gravy in the dish and serve it up with apple sauce and potatoes. A griskin roasted in this manner eats finely.

To Stuff a Chine of Pork

Make a stuffing of the fat leaf of pork, parsley, thyme, sage, eggs, and crumbs of bread; season it with pepper, salt, shalot and nutmeg, and stuff it thick, then roast it gently, and when it is about a quarter roasted, cut the skin in slips, and make your sauce with apples, lemon-peel, two or three cloves and a blade of mace; sweeten it with sugar, put some butter in and have mustard in a cup.

To Roast a Pig

Spit your pig and lay it down to a clear fire, kept good at both ends: Put into the belly a few sage leaves, a little pepper and salt, a little crust of bread, and a bit of butter, then sew up the belly; flour it all over very well, and do so till the eyes begin to start, when you find the skin is tight and crisp, and the eyes are dropp'd, put two plates into the dripping pan, to save what gravy comes from it: put a quar-

ter of a pound of butter into a clean course cloth, and rub all over it, till the flour is quite taken off; then take it up into your dish, take the sage, &c. out of the belly, and chop it small; cut off the head, open it, and take out the brains, which chop, and put the sage and brains into half a pint of good gravy, with a piece of butter rolled in flour; then cut your pig down the back, and lay it flat in the dish: Cut off the two ears, and lay one upon each shoulder: take off the under jaw, cut it in two, and lay one upon each side; put the head between the shoulders; pour the gravy out of the plates into your sauce and then into the dish. Send it to table garnished with lemon, and if you please pap sauce in a bason.

Game and Poultry

To Roast Venison

After the haunch of venison is spitted, take a piece of butter, and rub all over the fat, dust on a little flour, and sprinkle a little salt: Then take a sheet of writing paper, butter it well, and lay over the fat parts; put two sheets over that, and tie the paper on with small twine: Keep it well basted, and let there be a good soaking fire. If a large haunch, it will take full three hours to do it. Five minutes before you send it to table, take off the paper, dust it over with a little flour, and baste it with butter; let it go up with a good froth; put no gravy in the dish, but send it in one boat, and current jelly melted, in another.

A warming pan filled with coals from the fire and slipped between the bedclothes was most welcome on cold winter nights.

To Roast a Hare

Case and truss your hare, and then make a pudding thus: A quarter of a pound of beef suet minced fine; as much bread crumbs; the liver chopped fine; parsley and lemon-peel shred fine, season'd with pepper, salt and nutmeg. Moisten it with an egg, and put it into the hare; sew up the belly, and lay it down to a good fire: Let your dripping-pan be very clean, put into it a quart of milk, and six ounces of butter, and baste it with this till the whole is used: about five minutes before you take it up; dust on a little flour and baste with fresh butter, that it may go to table with a good froth. Put a little gravy in the dish, and the rest in a boat. Garnish your dish with lemon.

Rabbit trussed for roasting.

To Roast Rabbits

Baste them with good butter, and dredge them with a little flour. Half an hour will do them at a very quick clear fire; and, if they are very small, twenty minutes will do them. Take the livers with a little bunch of parsley and boil them, and then chop them very fine together. Melt some good butter, put half the liver and parsley into the butter; pour it into the dish, and garnish the dish with the other half. Let your rabbits be done of a fine light brown.

To Roast a Rabbit Hare Fashion

Lard a rabbit with bacon, put a pudding in its belly, and roast it as you do hare, and it eats very well. Send it in with gravy sauce.

To Roast a Turkey, Goose, Duck, Fowl &c.

When you roast a turkey, goose, fowl or chicken, lay them down to a good fire. Singe them clean with white paper, baste them with butter, and dust on fine flour. As to time, a large turkey will take an hour and twenty minutes; a middling one a full hour; a full grown goose, if young an hour, a large fowl three quarters of an hour; a middling one half an hour, and a small chicken twenty minutes; but this depends entirely on the goodness of your fire.

When your fowls are thoroughly plump, and the smoak draws from the breast to the fire, you may be sure that they are very near done. Then baste them with butter; dust on a very little flour, and as soon as they have a good froth, serve them up.

Geese and ducks are commonly seasoned with onion, sage, and a little pepper and salt.

A turkey, when roasted, is generally stuffed in the craw with force meat; or the following stuffing: Take a pound of veal, as much grated bread, half a pound of suet and beat very fine a little parsley, with a small matter of thyme, or savory, two cloves, half a nutmeg grated, a tea-spoon full of shred lemon peel, a little pepper and salt, and the yolks of two eggs.

Sauce for a turkey; Good gravy in a dish; and either bread, onion, or oyster sauce in a bason.

Sauce for a goose; A little good gravy in one bason, and some apple sauce in another.

For a duck; a little gravy in the dish and onions in a tea cup.

Sauce for fowl; Parsley and butter, or gravy in the dish, and either bread sauce, oyster sauce, or egg sauce in a bason.

Sauceboat and ladle.

A Fowl or Turkey Roasted with Chesnuts

Roast a quarter of a hundred of chesnuts, and peel them; save out eight or ten, the rest bruise in a mortar, with the liver of the fowl, a quarter of a pound of ham well pounded, sweet herbs and parsley chopped fine. Season it with mace, nutmeg, pepper and salt. Mix all these together, and put them into the belly of your fowl. Spit it and tie the neck and vent close. For the sauce take the rest of the chesnuts, cut them in pieces and put them into a strong gravy, with a glass of white wine; Thicken with a piece of butter rolled into flour. Pour the sauce in the dish and garnish with orange and water cresses.

To Roast a Green Goose with Green Sauce

Roast your goose nicely; in the mean time make your sauce thus: Take half a pint of the juice of sorrel, a spoonful of white wine, a little grated nutmeg, and some grated bread; boil this over a gentle fire, and sweeten it with pounded sugar to your taste; let your goose have a good froth on it before you take it up; put some good strong gravy in the dish, and the same in a boat. Garnish with lemon.

The passenger pigeon, a wild pigeon once so abundant that several millions might be in one flock. Audubon once watched a single flock in flight pass in a stream that lasted for three days and was so thick that it darkened the sun. As a result of hunters' greed and foolish waste, this bird is now extinct.

The German Way of Dressing Fowls

Take a turkey or fowl, stuff the breast with what force meat you like, fill the body with roasted chesnuts peeled and lay it down to roast: take half a pint of good gravy, with a little piece of butter rolled in flour: boil these together, with some small turnips and sausages cut in slices, and fried or boiled. Garnish with chesnuts.

Note: You may dress ducks the same way.

To Roast Pigeons

Take a little pepper and salt, a small piece of butter, and some parsley cut small; mix these together, put them into the bellies of your pigeons, tying the neck ends tight; take another string, fasten one end of it to their legs and rumps, and the other to the mantlepiece. Keep them constantly turning round, and baste them with butter. When they are done, take them up, lay them in a dish, and they will swim with gravy.

Wild Ducks, Widgeons, or Teals

Wild fowl are in general liked rather under done; and if your fire is very good and brisk, a duck or Widgeon will be done in a quarter of an hour; for as soon as they are well hot through, they begin to loose their gravy, and if not drawn off, will eat hard. A teal is done in a little more than ten minutes.

To Roast Woodcocks or Snipes

Spit them on a small bird spit; flour them, and baste them with butter: Have ready a slice of bread, toasted brown, which lay in a dish and set it under your birds for the trail to drop on. When they are enough, take them up, and lay them on the toast; put some good gravy in the dish and some melted butter in a cup. Garnish with orange or lemon.

Roasting small birds by hanging them before the fire on strings. The housewife twisted the strings from time to time to keep the birds turning.

To Roast Quails

Truss them, and stuff their bellies with beef suet and sweet herbs shred very fine, and seasoned with a little spice: When they grow warm, baste them with salt and water, then dredge them, and baste them with butter. For sauce, dissolve an anchovy in good gravy, with two or three shalots sliced very fine, and the juice of a Seville orange; dish them up in this sauce, and garnish your dish with fried bread crumbs, and lemon; send them to table as hot as possible.

To Roast Pheasants

Take a brace of pheasants, lard them with small lards of bacon: butter a piece of white paper, and put it over the breasts, and about ten minutes before they are done, take off the paper; flour and baste them with nice butter that they may go to the table with a fine froth. Put good gravy in the dish, and bread sauce as for partridges, in a boat; garnish your dish with lemon.

To Roast Partridges

When they are a little under roasted, dredge them in flour, and baste them with fresh butter: Let them go to table with a fine froth, and gravy sauce in the dish, and bread sauce in a bason. Make your bread sauce thus: take a good piece of stale bread and put it into a pint of water, with some whole pepper, a blade of mace, and a bit of onion: Let it boil till the bread is soft; then take out the spice and onion: pour out the water and beat the bread with a spoon till it is like pap; put in a good piece of butter and a little salt; set it over the fire for two or three minutes; then put it into your boat. Garnish your partridges with sliced orange or lemon.

To Roast Plovers

Green plovers are roasted as you do woodcocks: lay them upon a toast, and put good gravy sauce in the dish. Gray plovers are roasted, or stewed thus: Make a force meat of artichoke bottoms cut small, seasoned with pepper, salt, and nutmeg: Stuff the bellies and put the birds into a sauce pan with a good gravy just to cover them, a glass of white wine, and a blade of mace; cover them close, and stew them softly, till they are tender; then take up your plovers into the dish; put in a piece of butter, rolled in flour, to thicken your sauce; let it boil till smooth; squeeze in a little lemon; scum it clean, and pour it over the birds.

To Roast Larks

Truss your larks with the legs a cross, and put a large leaf over the breast; put them upon a long fine skewer, and between every lark a little piece of thin bacon, then tie the skewers to a spit, and roast them at a quick, clear fire, baste them with butter, and strew over them some crumbs of bread mixed with flour; fry some bread crumbs of a nice brown in a bit of butter; lay your larks round in your dish, the bread crumbs in the middle, with a sliced orange for garnish. Send good gravy in the dish.

To Roast Ortolans

You may lard them with bacon, or roast them without, putting a vine leaf between each; spit them side ways, baste them with buter, and strew bread crumbs on them while roasting: Send them to table with fried bread crumbs a round them, garnished with lemon, and a good gravy sauce in a boat.

To Dress Ruffs and Reeves

You may fatten them as you do chickens with white bread, milk and sugar: They feed fast, and will die in their fattening, if not killed in time. When you dress them, draw them and truss them cross legged, as you do snipes and spit them the same way; lay them upon a buttered toast, pour good gravy into the dish and serve them up quick.

Trade sign.

Of Fish

To Roast a Cod's Head

Take the head, wash and scour it very clean then scotch it with a knife, strew a little salt on it and lay it on a stew pan before the fire, with something behind it: throw away the water that runs from it the first half hour; then strew on it some nutmeg, cloves, mace, and salt, and baste it often with butter, turning it till it is enough. If it be a large head it will take four or five hours roasting; then take all the gravy of the fish, as much white wine, and more meat gravy, some horse-radish, one or two shalots, a little sliced ginger, some whole pepper, cloves, mace, and nutmeg, a bay leaf or two; boil this liquer up with butter, and the liver of the fish boiled, broke and strained into it, with the yolks of two or three eggs, oysters, shrimps, and balls made of fish; place fried fish round it. Garnish with lemon, and horse-radish.

To Roast a Pike

Take a large pike, gut it, clean it, and lard it in eel and bacon, as you lard a fowl; then take thyme, savory salt, mace, nutmeg, some crumbs of bread, beef suet and parsley, shred all very fine, and mix it up with raw eggs; make it in a long pudding, and put it in the belly of your pike; sew up the belly and dissolve three anchovies in butter to baste it with; put two splints on each side of the pike and tie it to the spit: melt butter thick for the sauce; or if you please, oyster sauce, and bruise the pudding in it. Garnish with lemon.

To Roast an Eel

Take a large eel and scour him well with salt; skin him almost to the tail; then gut wash, and dry him, take a quarter of a pound of suet, shred as fine as possible; put to it sweet herbs, a shallot likewise shred very fine, and mix them together, with some salt, pepper, and grated nutmeg; scotch your eel on both sides, the breadth of a fingers distance, wash it over with yolks of eggs; lay some seasoning over it, and stuff the belly with it; then draw the skin over it, put a long skewer through it and tie it to the spit, baste it with butter, and make the sauce of anchovies and butter melted.

Chap. II

Of Boiling

General Rules to Be Observed in Boiling

Be very careful that your pots and covers are well tinned, very clean, and free from sand. Mind that your pot really boils all the while; otherwise you will be disappointed in dressing any joint, though it has been a proper time over the fire. Fresh meat should be put in when the water boils, and salt meat whilst it is cold. Take care likewise to have sufficient room and water in the pot, and allow a quarter of an hour to every pound of meat, let it weigh more or less.

Butcher's Meat

To Boil Beef or Mutton

When your meat is put in, and the pot boils, take care to scum it very clean, otherwise the scum will boil down, stick to your meat, and make it look black. Send up your dish with turnips, greens, potatoes, or carrots. If it be a loin or leg of mutton, you may also put melted butter and capers in a boat.

To Boil a Leg of Pork

A leg of pork must lie in salt six or seven days; after which put it to the pot to be boiled, without using any means to freshen it. It requires much water to swim in over the fire, and also to be fully boiled; so that care should be taken, that the fire does not slacken while it is dressing. Serve it up with a pease pudding, melted butter, Durham mustard, buttered turnips, carrots or greens.

N.B. The other joints of the swine are most commonly roasted.

Boiling was the most common method of cooking. Pots required little attention, and so long as the water didn't waste away or the fire die, dinner went right on cooking.

To Boil Pickled Pork

Wash the pork, and scrape it clean. Put it in while the water is cold, and boil it till the rind be tender. It is to be served up always with boiled greens, and is most commonly itself a sauce to boiled fowls or veal.

To Boil Veal

Let the pot boil, and have a good fire when you put in the meat; be sure to scum it very clean. A knuckle of veal will take more boiling in proportion to its weight, than any other joint, because the beauty is to have all the gristles soft and tender.

   You may either send up boiled veal with parsley and butter; or with bacon and greens.

To Boil a Calf's Head

The head must be picked very clean, and soaked in a large pan of water, a considerable time before it be put into the pot. Tie the brains up in a rag, and put them into the pot well; then put in a piece of bacon, in proportion to the number of people to eat thereof. You will find it to be enough by the tenderness of the flesh about that part that joined to the neck. When enough you may grill it before the fire, or serve it up with melted butter, bacon and greens, and with the brains mashed and beat up with a little butter, salt, pepper, and sugar or lemon, sage, and parsley, in a separate plate; or serve the brains whole, and the tongue slit down the middle.

To Boil Lamb

A leg of lamb of five pounds will not be boiled in less than an hour and a quarter; and if, as it ought to be, it be boiled in a good deal of water, and your pot be kept clean scummed, you may dish it up as white as a curd. Send it to table in stewed spinach, and melted butter in a boat.

To Boil a Neat's Tongue

A dried tongue should be soaked over night, when you dress it put it in cold water, and let it have room; it will take at least four hours. A green tongue out of the pickle need not be soaked, but will require near the same time. An hour before you dish it up take it out and blanch it, then put it into the pot again till you want it, this will make it eat the tenderer.

Training calves to the yoke.

To Boil a Ham

A ham requires a great deal of water, therefore put it in the copper cold, and let it only simmer for two hours, and allow a full quarter of an hour to every pound of ham; by this means your ham will eat tender and well.

A dry ham should be soaked in water over night; a green one does not require soaking. Take care they are well cleaned before you dress them.

Before you send a ham to the table take off the rind, and sprinkle it over with bread crumbs, and put it in an oven for a quarter of an hour; or you may crisp it with a hot salamander.

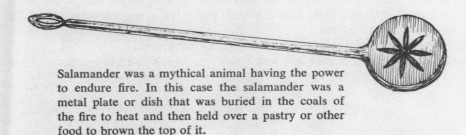

Salamander was a mythical animal having the power to endure fire. In this case the salamander was a metal plate or dish that was buried in the coals of the fire to heat and then held over a pastry or other food to brown the top of it.

To Boil a Haunch of Venison

Salt the haunch well, and let it lay a week; then boil it with a colliflower, some turnips, young cabbages, and beet roots. Lay your venison in the dish, dispose the garden things round it, and send it to table.

Game and Poultry

To Boil a Turkey, Fowl, Goose, Duck, &c.

Poultry are best boiled by themselves, and in a good deal of water; scum your pot clean, and you need not be afraid of their going to table of a bad colour. A large turkey, with a force meat in the craw, will take two hours; one without, an hour and a half; a hen turkey, three quarters of an hour; a large fowl, forty minutes; a small one, half an hour; a large chicken, twenty minutes, and a small one, a quarter of an hour. A full grown goose salted, an hour and a half; a large duck, near an hour.

Sauce for boiled turkey. Take a little water, a bit of thyme, an onion, a blade of mace, a little lemon peel, and an anchovy; boil these together, and strain them through a sieve, adding a little melted butter. Fry a few sausages to lay round the dish, and garnish with lemon.

Sauce for a fowl. Parsley and butter; or white oyster sauce.

For a goose. Onions or cabbage, first boiled and then stewed in butter for a few minutes.

Chicken Boiled with Cellery Sauce

Put two fine chickens into a sauce pan to boil, and in the mean time prepare the sauce; take the white part of two bunches of cellery, cut about an inch and a half long, and boil it till tender; strain off the water and put the cellery into a stew pan, with half a pint of cream, and a piece of butter rolled in flour; season with pepper and salt; set it over a clear fire, and keep it stirring till it is smooth, and of a good thickness. Have ready half a dozen rashers of bacon; take up your chickens, pour your sauce into the dish, and put the rashers of bacon, and sliced lemon round.

To Boil Pigeons

Let the pigeons be boiled by themselves for about a quarter of an hour; then boil a proper quantity of bacon, cut square, and lay it in the middle of the dish. Stew some spinach to put round, and lay the pigeons on the spinach. Garnish with parsley dried crisp before the fire.

To Boil Rabbits

Truss your rabbits close; boil them off white; for sauce, take the livers, which, when boiled, bruise with a spoon very fine, and take out all the strings; put to this some good broth, a little parsley shred fine, and some barberries clean pick'd from the stalks; season it with mace and nutmeg, thicken it with a piece of butter rolled in flour, and a little white wine. Let your sauce be of a good thickness, and pour it over the rabbits. Garnish with lemon and barberries.

To Boil Rabbits with Onions

Truss your rabbits short with the head turned over their shoulders; Let them be boiled off very white. Boil some large onions in a good deal of water, till they are very tender; put them into a cullinder and when drained, pass them through it with a good piece of butter, a little salt, and a gill of cream: Stir them over the fire till they are of a good thickness; then dish up your rabbits, and pour the onions over them. Garnish with bacon and raw parsley.

To Boil Woodcocks or Snipes

Boil them either in beef gravy, or good strong broth made in the best manner; put your gravy, when made to your mind, into a sauce-pan, and season with salt; take the guts of your snipes out clean, and put them into your gravy, and let them boil; let them be covered close, and kept boiling, and then ten minutes will be sufficient. In the mean time, cut the guts and liver small. Take a small quantity of the liquor your snipes are boiled in, and stew the guts with a blade of mace. Take some crumbs of bread (about the quantity of the inside of a stale roll) and have them ready fried crisp in a little fresh butter; when they are done, let them stand ready in a place before the fire. When your snipes or woodcocks are ready, take about half a pint of the liquor they are boiled in, and put in two spoonfuls of red wine to the guts, and a lump of butter rolled in flour, about as big as a walnut: set them on the fire in a sauce pan. Never stir it with a spoon, but shake it well till the butter is all melted; then put in your crumbs; shake your saucepan well; then take your birds up, and pour your sauce over them.

To Boil Pheasants

Let them be dressed in a good deal of water, if large, three quarters of an hour will do them, if small, half an hour. For sauce, use stewed cellery, thickened with cream, and a piece of butter rolled in flour, a little salt and nutmeg grated, and a spoonful of white wine; pour the sauce over them; and garnish with orange cut in quarters.

To Boil Partridges

Boil them quick, and in a good deal of water; a quarter of an hour will do them.

For sauce, parboil the livers and scald some parsley: chop these fine; and put them into some melted butter; squeeze in a little lemon, and give it a boil up, and pour it over the birds. Garnish with lemon.

But this is a more elegant Sauce: Take a few mushrooms, fresh peeled, and wash them clean, put them in a sauce-pan with a little salt, set them over a quick fire, let them boil up, then put in a quarter of a pint of cream, and a little nutmeg; shake them together with a very little piece of butter rolled in flour, give it two or three shakes over the fire, three or four minutes will do; then pour it over the birds.

Of Fish

To Boil a Turbot

A turbot ought to be put into pump water, with salt and vinegar, for two hours before it is dressed. In the mean time, put a sufficiency of water into a fish kettle, with a stick of horse-raddish sliced, a handful of salt, and a faggot of sweet herbs. When the water tastes of the seasoning, take it off the fire, and let it cool a little, to prevent the fish from breaking. Put a handful of salt into the mouth and belly of the turbot, put it into the kettle, and boil it gently; a middling turbot will take about twenty minutes.

Sauce: Lobster sauce, anchovy sauce, and plain butter in separate basons.

To Boil a Cod

Gut and wash the fish very clean inside and out, and rub the backbone with a handful of salt; put it upon a fish plate, and boil it gently till it be enough; and remember always to boil the liver along with it. Garnish with scraped horse-radish, small fried fish and and sliced lemon.

Sauce: Oyster sauce, shrimp sauce, or lobster sauce, with plain melted butter in different boats, and mustard in a tea cup.

To Boil a Cod's Head

After tying your cod's head round with pack-thread to keep it from flying, put a fish-kettle on the fire, large enough to cover it with water; put in some salt, a little vinegar, and some horse-radish sliced; when the water boils, lay your fish upon a drainer, and put it into the kettle; let it boil gently till it rises to the surface of the water, which it will do, if your kettle is large enough; then take it out, and set it to drain; slide it carefully off your drainer into your fish plate. Garnish with lemon, and horse-radish scraped.

Have oyster sauce in one bason, and shrimp sauce in another.

Cod's head.

To Boil Crimp Cod

Cut a cod into slices, and throw it into pump water and salt; set over your stove a large fish kettle, or turbot pan, almost full of spring water, and salt sufficient to make it brackish; let it boil quick, then put in your slices of cod, and keep it boiling and clean scum'd; in about eight minutes the fish will be enough; then take the slices carefully up, and lay them on a fish plate. Garnish your dish with horse-radish, lemon and raw parsley.

Send shrimp sauce in one boat, and oyster sauce in one other.

You may, if you please, take some of the largest slices, flour them and broil them to a fine brown, and send them in a dish for the lower end of the table.

To Boil Scate

Great care must be taken in cleaning this fish, and as it is commonly too large to be boiled in a pan at once, the best way is to cut it into long slips cross ways, about an inch broad and throw it into salt and water and if the water boils quick it will be enough in three minutes. Drain it well and serve it up with butter and mustard in one bason and anchovy sauce in another.

You may, if you please place spitchcock'd eels, round about the scate.

Boot scrapers.

To Boil Soals

Clean the soals well, and having laid them two hours in vinegar, salt and water, dry them in a cloth, and then put them into a fish pan with an onion, some whole pepper, and a little salt. Cover the pan and let them boil till enough. Serve them up with anchovy sauce, and butter melted plain; or with shrimp or muscle sauce.

To Boil Plaice and Flounders

Let the pan boil; throw some salt into the water; then put in the fish; and (being boiled enough) take it out with a slice, and drain it well. Serve it up with parsley boiled, to garnish the edges of the dish; and with a bason of butter melted plain, and anchovy sauce, or butter melted with a little catchup.

A fish slice was a rather flat, pierced, spatulalike tool used to lift pieces of cooked fish.

To Boil Sturgeon

Having cleaned the sturgeon well, boil it in as much liquor as will just barely cover it, adding two or three bits of lemon-peel, some whole pepper, a stick of horse-radish, and a pint of vinegar, to every two quarts of water. When it is enough, garnish the dish with fried oysters, sliced lemon, and a scraped horse-radish; and serve it up with sufficient quantity of melted fresh butter, with cavear dissolved in it; or (where that is not to be had) with anchovy sauce, and with the body of a crab bruised in the butter, and a little lemon-juice, served up in basons.

To Boil Salmon

Let it be well scraped and cleansed from scales and blood; and after it has lain about an hour in salt and spring water, put it into a fish kettle, with a proportionate quantity of salt and horse-radish, and a bunch of sweet herbs. Put it in while the water is lukewarm, and boil it gently till enough, or about half an hour, if it be thick; or twenty minutes, if it be a small piece. Pour off the water, dry it well, and dish it nicely upon a fish plate, in the center, and garnish the dish with horse-radish scraped, (as is done for roast beef,) or with fried smelts or gudgeons, and with slices of lemon round the rim.

The sauce to be melted butter, with or without anchovy, shrimp or lobster sauce, in different basons, served up with the fish.

Pot rest.

To Boil Carp

Take a brace of large carp, scale them and slit the tails, let them bleed into about half a pint of red wine, with half a nutmeg grated; (keep it stirring, or the blood will congeal) then gut and wash them very clean; boil the roes first, and then the carp, as you would do any other fish, then fry them; take some sippets cut corner ways; dip some large oysters in butter, and fry them also, of a fine brown.

For the sauce, take two anchovies, a piece of lemon-peel, a little horse-radish, and a bit of onion; boil these in water till the anchovies are wasted; strain the liquor into a clean sauce-pan, and, as you like, the oysters stewed, and a lobster cut small, without the spawn, craw-fish, or shrimps; set it over the fire, and let it boil; then take near a pound of butter, roll a good piece in flour, put it into your sauce-pan with the liquor, with what other ingredients you intend, and boil all together, till it is of a good thickness; then pour in the wine and blood, and shake it about, letting it only simmer, take up the fish, put them into a dish, and pour the sauce over them.

Garnish your dish with fried oysters, horse-radish, fried parsley and lemon; stick the sippets about the fish, and lay the roe, some on the fish, and the rest in a dish; send it to table as hot as you can.

To Boil Tench

Clean your tench very well then put them into a stew-pan, with as much water as will cover them; put in some salt, whole pepper, lemon-peel, horse-radish, and a bundle of sweet herbs, and boil them till they are enough.

Take some of the liquor, a glass of white wine, a pint of shrimps, and an anchovy bruised; boil all together in a sauce-pan, roll a good piece of butter in flour, and brake it into the sauce; when of a proper thickness, pour it over the dish. Garnish with lemon and horse-radish scraped.

To Boil Mackral

Having cleansed the mackral very well, and soaked them for some time in spring water, put them and the roes into a stew pan with as much water as will cover them, and little salt, and a small bunch of fennel along with them, and when you send them up, garnish with the roes, and the fennel shred fine.

Sauce: Grated sugar in a saucer; melted butter, and green gooseberries boiled, in different basons, or, parsley and butter, with a little vinegar.

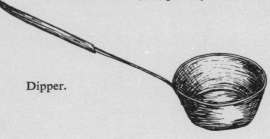

Dipper.

To Boil Eels

Having skinned and washed your eels, and cut off the back fins with a pair of scissors, roll them round with the heads innermost and run a strong skewer through them. Put them into a stew-pan with a sufficient quantity of water, and a little vinegar and salt. Garnish with sliced lemon.

Sauce: Parsley and butter.

To Boil Pike or Jack

Gut and clean your pike very well with salt and water; fasten the tail in the mouth with a skewer; then put them into a stew pan with as much water as will cover it, a little vinegar and salt, and a piece of horse-radish sliced. Garnish with sliced lemon, and scraped horse-radish.

Sauce: Anchovy or shrimp sauce; or melted butter and catchup.

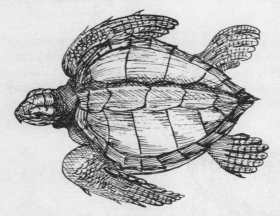

The large Atlantic turtle made a tasty stew.

To Dress a Turtle

Fill a boiler or kettle with a quantity of water sufficient to scald the callapach and callapee, the fins, &c. And about nine o'clock hang up your turtle by the hind fins, cut off its head, and save the blood; then with a sharp pointed knife separate the callapach from the callapee (or the back from the belly part) down to the shoulders, so as to come at the entrails, which take out, and clean them, as you would those of any other animal, and throw them into a tub of clean water, taking great care not to break the gall, but to cut it off the liver, and throw it away. Then separate each distinctly, and take the guts into another vessel, open them with a fine pen knife from end to end, wash them clean, and draw them through a woolen cloth in warm water, to clear away the slime, and then put them into clean cold water till they are used, with the other part of the entrails, which must all be cut up small to be mixed in the baking dishes with the meat. This done, separate the back and the belly pieces entirely, cutting away the four fins by the upper joint, which scald, peel off the loose skin, and cut them into small pieces, laying them by themselves, either in another vessel, or on the table, ready to be seasoned.

Then cut off the meat from the belly part, and clean the back from the lungs, kidneys, &c. and that meat cut into pieces as small as a walnut, laying it likewise by itself. After this you are to scald the back and belly pieces, pulling off the shell from the back, and the yellow skin from the belly; when all will be white and clean, and with the kitchen cleaver cut those up likewise into pieces, about the bigness or breadth of a card. Put those pieces into clean cold water, wash them out, and place them in a heap on the table, so that each part may lay by itself.

The meat, being thus prepared and laid separate for seasoning, mix two-thirds parts of salt, or rather more, and one-third part of Cayenne pepper, black pepper, and a nutmeg and mace pounded fine, and mixed together; the quantity to be proportioned to the size of the turtle, so that in each dish there may be about three spoonfuls of seasoning to every twelve pounds of meat.

Your meat being thus seasoned, get some sweet herbs, such as thyme, savory, &c. Let them be dried and rubbed fine, and having provided some deep dishes to bake it in, (which should be of the common brown ware) put in the coarsest parts of the meat at the bottom, with about a quarter of a pound of butter in each dish, and then some of each of the several parcels of meat, so that the dishes may all be alike, and have equal portions of the different parts of the turtle; and between each layering of the meat, strew a little of the mixture of sweet herbs. Fill your dishes within an inch and a half, or two inches of the top; boil the blood of the turtle, and put into it; then lay on force-meat balls made of veal, or fowl, highly seasoned with the same seasoning as the turtle; put in each dish a gill of good Madeira wine, and as much water as it will conveniently hold; then break over it five or six eggs, to keep the meat from scorching at the top, and over that shake a handful of shred parsley, to make it look green; which done, put your dishes into an oven made hot enough to bake bread, and in an hour and a half, or two hours, (according to the size of your dishes) it will be sufficiently done.

To Boil All Kinds of GARDEN STUFF

In dressing all sorts of kitchen garden herbs, take care they are clean washed; that there be no small snails, or caterpillars between the leaves; and that all the coarse outer leaves, and the tops that have received any injury by the weather, be taken off. Next wash them in a good deal of water, and put them into a cullender to drain. Care must likewise be taken, that your pot or sauce-pan be clean, well tinned, and free from sand, or grease.

To Boil Asparagus

First cut the white ends off about six inches from the head, and scrape them from the green part downward very clean. As you scrape them, throw them into a pan of clean water; and after a little soaking, tie them up in small even bundles, when your water boils, put them in, and boil them up quick; but by over boiling they will loose their heads. Cut a slice of bread for a toast, and bake it brown on both sides. When your grass is done, take them up carefully; dip the toast in the asparagus water, and lay it in the bottom of your dish; then lay the heads of the asparagus on it, with the white ends downwards; pour a little melted butter over the heads; cut an orange in small quarters and stick them between for garnish.

Artichoke.

To Boil Artichokes

Wring off the stalks close to the artichokes; throw them into water and wash them clean; then put them into a pot or sauce-pan. They will take better than an hour after the water boils; but the best way is to take out a leaf, and if it draws easy, they are enough. Send them to table with butter in tea-cups between each artichoke.

To Boil Colliflower

A colliflower is the most favorite plant in the kitchen garden, amongst the generality of people. Take off all the green part, and cut the flower close at the bottom from the stalk; and if it be large or dirty, cut it into four quarters, that it may lay better in the pan, and be thoroughly cleansed. Let it soak an hour, if possible, in clear water, and then put it into boiling milk and water, (if you have any milk) or water only, and skim the pan well. When the flower or stalk left about it feel tender, it will be enough; but it must be taken up before it loses its crispness; for colliflower is good for nothing that boils till it becomes quite soft. When enough, lay it to drain in a cullender for a minute or two, and serve it up in a dish by itself, and with melted butter in a bason.

To Boil Broccoli

Strip off the small branches from the great one, then with a knife peel off the hard outside skin, till you come to the top, which is on the stalks and small branches, and throw them into a pan of clear water as you do them. Have water boiling in a stew-pan with some salt in it; when it boils put in your broccoli, and as soon as the stalks are tender, they are enough. Take them up with a skimmer, and be careful you do not break the heads off.

Some eat broccoli like asparagus, with a toast baked, and laid to the dish, with the broccoli upon it, and sent to table with a little melted butter poured over it.

To Boil French Beans

Take your beans and string them; cut them in two and then a cross, when you have done them all, sprinkle them over with salt, and stir them together. As soon as your water boils, put them in, salt and all; make them boil up quick. They will be soon done, and look of a better green than when growing in the garden. If they are very young, only take off the ends, break them in two, and dress them in the same manner.

The broad bean.

To Boil Broad Beans

Beans require a good deal of water, and it is best not to shell them till just before they are ready to go into the pot. When the water boils, put them in with some pick'd parsley, and some salt: Make them boil up quick, and when you see them begin to fall, they are enough. Strain them off. Garnish the dish with boiled parsley, and send plain butter in a cup, or boat.

To Boil Green Pease

When your pease are shelled, and the water boils, which should not be much more than will cover them, put them in with a few leaves of mint: As soon as they boil, throw a piece of butter as big as a walnut, and stir them about; when they are enough, strain them off, and sprinkle on a little salt; shake them till the water drains off; send them hot to table, with melted butter in a cup.

To Boil Cabbage

If your cabbage is large, cut it into quarters; if small, cut it in half; let your water boil, then put in a little salt and next your cabbage, with a little more salt upon it; make your water boil as soon as possible, and when the stalk is tender, take up your cabbage into a cullender, or sieve, that the water may drain off, and send it to table as hot as you can. Savoys are dressed in the same manner.

To Boil Sprouts

Pick and wash your sprouts very clean, and see there are no snails or grubs between the leaves, cut them a cross the stem, but not the heart; after they are well washed, take them out of the water to drain; when your water boils, put in some salt, and then the sprouts, with a little more salt on them; Make them boil quick, and if any scum arises take it clean off. As soon as the stalks are tender, strain them off, or they will not only lose their colour, but likewise their flavour.

To Boil Spinach

There is no herb requires more care in the washing than spinach; you must carefully pick it leaf by leaf, take off the stalks, and wash it in three or four waters; then put it into a cullender to drain. It does not require much water to dress it: half a pint, in a sauce pan that holds two quarts, will dress as much spinach as is generally wanted for a small family. When your water boils put in your spinach

Green pea.

with a small handful of salt, pressing it down with the spoon, as you put it into the sauce-pan; let it boil quick, and as soon as tender, put it into a sieve or cullender, and press out all the water. When you send it to table, raise it up with a fork, that it may lay hallow in the dish.

To Boil Turnips

A great deal depends upon preparing this root for boiling. They require paring till all the stringy coat be cut quite off: for that outside will never boil tender. Being well rinded, cut them in two, and boil them in the pot with either beef, mutton, or lamb. When they become tender, take them out, press the liquor from them between two trenchers, put them into a pan, and mash them with butter and a little salt, and send them to table in a plate or bason by themselves. Or send them out of the pot in a plate, with some melted butter in a bason, for every one to butter and season them, as they like.

Coffee grinder.

To Boil Parsnips

Parsnips are a very sweet root, and an agreeable sauce for salt fish. They should be boiled in a great deal of water, and when you find they are soft (which is known by running a fork into them) take them up and carefully scrape all the dirt off them, and then with a knife scrape them all fine, throwing away all the dirty parts; then put them in a sauce-pan with some milk, and stir them over the fire till they are thick. Take care they do not burn; add a good piece of butter, and a little salt, and when the butter is melted send them to table.

But common parsnips are served up in a dish, when well boiled and scraped, with melted butter in a bason.

To Boil Carrots

Let them be scraped very clean, and when they are enough, rub them in a clean cloth, then slice some of them into a plate and pour some melted butter over them; and garnish the dish with the others, either whole or cut into pieces, or split down the middle. If they are young spring carrots, half an hour will boil them; if large, an hour; but old Sandwich carrots will take two hours.

To Boil Potatoes

Potatoes must always be peeled, except they be very small and new, then some people fancy to eat them skin and all. Some pare potatoes before they are put into the pot; others think it the best way both for having time and preventing waste, to peel off the skin as soon as they are boiled; which then slips off by rubbing them with a coarse cloth. In boiling of them take care they be enough, and not over done; for if boiled too much, they mash and become watery. Therefore it requires good attention when you are boiling potatoes, and that they be taken up as soon as they begin to shew the least disposition to break. This is a root in great request, and served up in a dish or plate, whole for the most part, with a bason of melted butter. On which occasion, it will be some addition to the potatoes to set them before the fire till they are quite dry, and a little browned.

Adjustable crane with a trammel holding the iron pot.

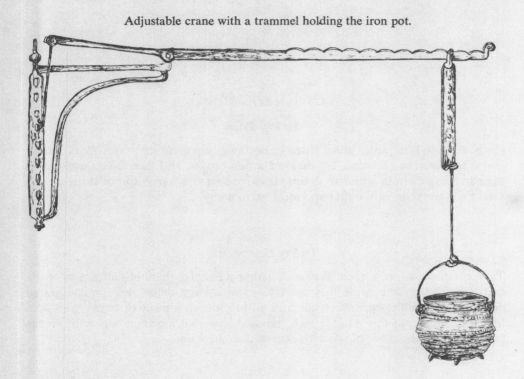

Chap. III

Of Frying

Of Butcher's Meat

To Fry Tripe

Cut your tripe into pieces about three inches long, dip them into the yolk of an egg and a few crumbs of bread, fry them of a fine brown, and then take them out of the pan & lay them in a dish to drain. Have ready a warm dish to put them in, and send them to table, with butter and mustard in a cup.

To Fry Beef Steaks

Take rump steaks, beat them very well with a roller; fry them in half a pint of ale that is not bitter, and while they are frying cut a large onion small, some grated nutmeg, and a little pepper and salt; roll all together in a piece of butter, and then in a little flour; put this into the stew pan and shake all together. When the steaks are tender and the sauce of a fine thickness, dish them up.

Another Way to Fry Beef Steaks

Cut the lean by itself, and beat them well with the back of a knife; fry them in just so much butter as will moisten the pan, pour out the gravy as it runs out of the meat; turn them often, and do them over a gentle fire; then fry the fat by itself, and lay upon the lean, and put to the gravy a glass of red wine, half an anchovy, a little nutmeg, a little beaten pepper, and a shallot cut small; give it two or three little boils, season it with salt to your palate, pour it over the steaks and send them to table.

To Fry a Loin of Lamb

Cut the loin into thin steaks, put a very little pepper and salt, and a little nutmeg on them, and fry them in fresh butter; when enough take out the steaks, lay them in a dish before the fire to keep hot; then pour out the butter, shake a little flour over the bottom of the pan, pour in a quarter of a pint of boiling water, and put a piece of butter; shake all together, give it a boil or two up, pour it over the steaks, and send it to table.

Note: You may do mutton the same way, and add two spoonfulls of walnut pickles.

Mutton for food, wool for clothing, and tallow for candles made the sheep a highly prized animal in the colonies.

To Fry Sausages with Apples

Take half a pound of sausages, and six apples; slice four about as thick as a crown, cut the other two in quarters, fry them with the sausages of a fine light brown, and lay sausages in the middle of the dish, and the apples round. Garnish with the quartered apples.

Stewed cabbages and sausages fried is a good dish; then heat cold peas pudding in the pan, lay it in the dish, and the sausages round, heap the pudding in the middle, and lay the sausages all round edge ways, and one in the middle at length.

To Fry Cold Veal

Cut it into pieces about as thick as half a crown, and as long as you please; dip them in the yolk of an egg, and then in crumbs of bread, with a few sweet herbs, and shred lemon peel in it; grate a little nutmeg over them, and fry them in fresh butter. The butter must be hot, and just enough to fry them in: In the mean time, make a little gravy of the bone of the veal; when the meat is fried, take it out with a fork, and lay it in a dish before the fire, then shake a little flour into the pan, and stir it round; put in a little gravy, squeeze in a little lemon, and pour it over the veal. Garnish with lemon.

A bellows blew air into the fire and not only helped to get it started, but made it give more heat once it was burning.

To Fry Beef Collops

Cut your beef in thin slices, about two inches long, lay them upon your dresser, and hack them with the back of a knife; grate a little nutmeg over them, and dust on some flour; lay them into a stew pan, and put in as much water as you think sufficient for sauce; shred half an onion, and a little lemon-peel very fine; add a bundle of sweet herbs, and a little pepper and salt; Roll a piece of butter in flour, and set them over a clear fire till they begin to simmer; shake them together often, but don't let them boil up; when they begin to simmer, ten minutes will do them; take out your herbs, and dish them up. Garnish the dish with pickles and horse-radish.

Pot rest.

To Make Scotch Collops

Dip the pieces of lean veal in the yolks of eggs, that have been beaten up with melted butter, a little salt, some grated nutmeg, and grated lemon-peel. Fry them quick; shake them all the time, to keep the butter from spoiling. Then put them to some beef gravy, and some mushrooms, or forced meat balls. Garnish with sausages and sliced lemon, and slices of broiled or fried bacon.

Observe, if you would have the collops white, do not dip them in eggs. And when fried tender, but not brown, pour off the liquor quite clean, and put in some cream to the meat, and give it just a boil up.

To Fry Veal Cutlets

Cut a neck of veal into steaks, and fry them in butter; and having made a strong broth of the scrag-end, boiled with two anchovies, some nutmeg, some lemon-peel, and parsley shred very small, and browned with a little burnt butter, put the cutlets and a glass of white wine into this liquor. Toss them up together; thicken with a bit of butter rolled in flour; and dish all together. Squeeze a Seville orange over, and strew as much salt on as shall give a relish.

To Fry Mutton Cutlets

Take a handful of grated bread, a little thyme and parsley, and lemon peel shred very small, with some nutmeg, pepper and salt; then take a loin of mutton, cut it into steaks; and let them be well beaten; then take the yolks of two eggs, rub all over the steaks: Strew on the grated bread with these ingredients mixed together. Make a sauce of gravy, with a spoonful or two of claret and a little anchovy.

To Fry Calf's Liver and Bacon

Cut the liver in slices and fry it first brown and nice, and then the bacon; lay the liver in the dish, and the bacon upon it. Serve it up with gravy and butter, and a little orange or lemon juice, and garnish with sliced lemon.

To Fry Sweetbreads and Kidneys

After splitting the kidneys, fry them and the sweetbreads in butter. Serve them up with a brown ragout sauce, and mushrooms; garnished with fried parsley and sliced lemon.

To Fry Eggs as Round as Balls

Having a deep frying pan, and three pints of clarified butter, heat it as hot as for fritters, and stir it with a stick, till it runs round like a whirlpool; then break an egg into the middle, and turn it round with your stick, till it be as hard as a poached egg; the whirling round of the butter will make it as round as a ball, then take it up with a slice, and put it in a dish before the fire; they will keep hot half an hour, and yet be soft; so you may do as many as you please. You may poach them in boiling water in the same manner.

Ice skate.

To Fry Carp

Scale and clean your carp very well. Cut them in two, sprinkle them with salt, flour them, and fry them in clarified butter. Make a ragout with a good fish broth, the melts of your fish, artichoke bottoms cut in small dice, and half a pint of shrimps; thicken it with the yolks of eggs, or a piece of butter rolled in flour; pour the ragout into a dish and lay your fried carp upon it. Garnish with fried sippets, crisp parsley, and lemon.

To Fry Tench

Slime your tenches, slip the skin along the backs, and with the point of your knife raise it up from the bone, then cut the skin accross at the head and tail and strip it off, and take out the bone; then take another trench or a carp, and mince the fish small with mushrooms, chives, and parsley. Season them with salt, pepper, beaten mace, nutmeg, and a few savory herbs minced small. Mingle these all well together, then pound them in a mortar, with crumbs of bread, as much as two eggs, and a piece of butter. When these have been well pounded, stuff the tenches with this sauce: Take clarified butter, and put it into a pan, set it over the fire, and when it is hot flour your tenches, and put them into the pan one by one, and fry them brown; then take them up, lay them in a coarse cloth before the fire, to keep hot. In the mean time, pour all the grease and fat out of the pan, put in a quarter of a pound of butter, shake some flour all over the pan, keep stirring with a spoon till the butter is a little brown; then pour in half a pint of white wine, stir it together, pour in half a pint of boiling water, an onion stuck with cloves, a bundle of sweet herbs, and a blade or two of mace. Cover them close, and let them stew as softly as you can for a quarter of an hour, then strain off the liquor, put it into the pan again, add two spoonfuls of catchup, have ready an ounce of truffles or morels boiled in half a pint of water tender, pour in the truffles water and all, into the pan, a few mushrooms, and either half a pint of oysters, clean washed in their own liquor, or some craw-fish; but then you must put in the tails; and after clean picking them, boil them in half a pint of water, then strain the liquor and put into the sauce; or take some fresh melts, and dish up your sauce. All this is just as you fancy.

When you find your sauce is very good, put your tench into the pan, make them quite hot, then lay them into your dish, and pour the sauce over them. Garnish with lemon.

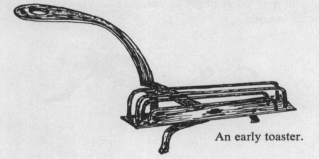

An early toaster.

To Fry Trout

Scale your trout clean, then gut them, and take out the gills, wash them, and dry them in a cloth, flour them, and fry them in butter, till they are of a fine brown; when they are enough, take them up, and serve them; fry some parsley green and crisp, melt anchovy and butter, with a spoonful of white wine. Dish your fish, and garnish with fried parsley, an sliced lemon. You may pour your sauce over the fish, or send it in a boat which you please.

In this manner you may fry perch, small pike, jacks, roach, gudgeons, or chine of fresh salmon.

To Fry Flat Fish

Dry the fish well in a cloth, rub them over with the yolk of an egg, and dust over some flour, let your oil, butter, lard, or drippings, be ready to boil before you put in the fish; try them off with a quick fire and let them be of a fine brown. Before you dish them up, lay them upon a drainer before the fire sloping, for two or three minutes, which will prevent their eating greasy.

You must observe on fast-days, and in *Lent,* never to dress your fish in any thing but butter, or oil.

To Fry Herrings

After having cleaned your herrings, take out the roes, dry them and the herrings in a cloth; flour them, and fry them in butter of a fine brown; lay them before the fire to drain; slice three or four onions, flour them, and fry them nicely; dish up the herrings, and garnish them with the roes and onions: Send them up as hot as you can, with butter and mustard in a cup.

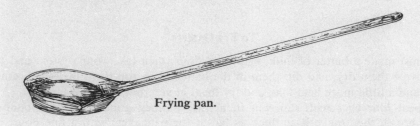

Frying pan.

To Fry Eels

After having cleaned and skinned your eels, split them, and cut them in pieces; let them lay for two or three hours in a pickle made of vinegar, salt, pepper, bay leaves, sliced onion, and juice of lemon; then dredge them well with flour, and fry them in clarified butter; serve them dry with dried parsley, and lemon for garnish. Send plain butter in a cup.

To Fry Lampries

Bleed them, and save the blood, then wash them in hot water, to take off the slime, cut them in pieces, and let them be fried in butter, not quite enough; drain out all the fat, then put in a little white wine, and shake your pan; season them with pepper, nutmeg, salt, sweet herbs, and a bay leaf, a good piece of butter rolled in flour, and the blood that was saved; cover them close, and shake the pan often. When you think they are enough, take them up, and give the sauce a quick boil, squeeze in a little lemon, and pour the sauce over the fish; send it to table. Garnish with lemon.

To Fry Small Fish of All Sorts

Small fish are generally dressed to garnish a dish of fish, as smelts, gudgeons, roach, small whitings, &c. Wipe them dry with a cloth, then rub them over with the yolk of an egg, flour them, and fry them in oil, butter, hogs lard, or beef drippings; take care they are fried of a fine light brown, and if they are sent by themselves in a dish, garnish with fried parsley and a lemon.

Whitings, when small, should be turned round, the tail put in the mouth, and be fried; if large, they are skinned, and turned round and fried.

Plaise, flounders, and dabs, are rubbed over with eggs, and fried.

Small maids are frequently dipped in butter, and fried.

All these sorts of fish are generally dressed by themselves for supper, you may send various sauces as you like, either shrimps, oysters, anchovy and butter, or plain melted butter, and some acate oil and lemon.

To Fry Oysters

You must make a batter of milk, eggs, and flour; then take your oysters and wash them, wipe them dry, and dip them in the batter; then roll them in some crumbled bread and a little mace beat fine, and fry them in very hot butter or lard.

Or beat four eggs with salt, put in a little nutmeg grated, and a spoonful of grated bread; then make it as thick as batter for pancakes, with a fine flour; drop the oysters in, and fry them brown in clarified beef suet. They are to lie round any dish of fish; ox palates boiled tender, blanched, and cut in pieces, then fried in such batter, is proper to garnish hashes or fricassees.

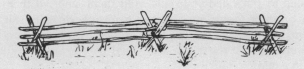

Of Garden Stuff

To Fry Artichoke Bottoms

First blanch them in water, then flour them, fry them in fresh butter, lay them in your dish, and pour melted butter over them. Or you may put a little red wine into the butter, and season with nutmeg, pepper and salt.

To Fry Colliflowers

Take two fine colliflowers, boil them in milk and water, then leave one whole, and pull the other to pieces; take half a pound of butter with two spoonfuls of water, a little dust of flour, and melt the butter in a stew-pan; then put in the whole colliflower cut in two, and the other pulled to pieces, and fry it till it is of a very light brown. Season it with pepper and salt. When it is enough, lay the two halves in the middle and pour the rest all over.

To Fry Cellery

Take six or eight heads of cellery, cut off the green tops, and take off the outside stalks, wash them clean; then have ready half a pint of white wine, the yolks of three eggs beat fine, and a little salt and nutmeg; mix all well together with flour in a batter, dip every head into the batter, and fry them in butter. When enough, lay them in the dish, and put melted butter over them.

To Fry Potatoes

Cut them into thin slices, as big as a crown piece, fry them brown, lay them in the plate or dish, pour melted butter, and sack and sugar over them. These are a pretty dinner plate.

An early one-hand wooden plow.

To Fry Onions

Take some large onions, peel them and cut them into slices about a quarter of an inch thick; then dip these slices into batter or an egg beaten, without breaking them and fry them of a nice brown.

To Fry Parsley

Pick the parsley very clean, and the best is very young. Then put a little butter into a clean pan, and when it is very hot put in the parsley; keep it stirring with a knife till it be crisp, then take it out, and use it as garnish to fried lamb &c.

Chap. IV

Of Broiling

To Broil Beef Steaks, Mutton or Pork Chops

Season the steak with a mixture of pepper and salt, and lay it on the gridiron. Do not turn the steak till one side be enough; and when the other side has been turned a little while, a fine gravy will lie on top of it; which you must take care to preserve; and lift it altogether with a pair of small tongs, or carefully with a knife and fork, into a hot dish, and put a little piece of butter under it, which will help to draw out the gravy. Some palates like it with a shallot or two, or an onion, shred very fine in the dish or plate.

But if they be mutton or pork steaks, they must be turned quick on the gridiron.

The general sauce for steaks is horse-radish for beef; mustard for pork; and girkins pickled for mutton. But in the season, I would recommend a good sallad, or green cucumber, or cellery for beef or mutton, and green peas for lamb steaks. All which sauces are served up in saucers, or plates &c. seperate from the meat.

To Broil Pigeons

Put a bit of butter, some shred parsleys and a little pepper and salt into the bellies of the pigeons, and tie them up neck and vent. Set your gridiron high, that they

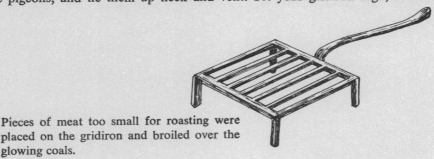

Pieces of meat too small for roasting were placed on the gridiron and broiled over the glowing coals.

may not burn, and have a little melted butter in a cup. You may split them and broil them with a little pepper and salt; and you may roast them only with a little parsley and butter in a dish.

Covey of grouse.

To Broil Chickens

Slit them down the back, and season them with pepper and salt, lay them on a very clear fire, and at a very great distance. Let the inside be next to the fire, till it is about half done; then turn them, and take great care the fleshy side do not burn; throw some fine raspings of bread over it, and let them be of a fine brown, but not burnt. Let your sauce be good gravy, with mushrooms, and garnish with lemon and the livers broiled, the gizzards cut, slashed, and broiled with pepper and salt.

To Broil Cod, Salmon, Whiting, or Haddock

Flour them and have a quick clear fire; set your gridiron high; broil them of a fine brown; lay them in a dish and for sauce have good melted butter. Take a lobster, bruise the body in the butter, cut the meat small, put all together into the melted butter, make it hot and pour it into the dish, or into basons. Garnish with horse-radish and lemon.

To Broil Mackrel

Cut off their heads, gut them, wash them clean; pull out the roe at the neck end, boil it in a little water, then bruise it with a spoon, beat up the yolk of an egg, with a little nutmeg, a little lemon peel cut fine, a little thyme, some parsley boiled and chopped fine, a little pepper and salt, and a few crumbs of bread; mix all well together, and fill the mackrel; flour it well, and broil it nicely. Let your sauce be plain butter, with a little catchup or walnut pickle.

To Broil Herrings

Scale them, gut them, cut off their heads, wash them clean, dry them in a cloth; flour them and broil them, but with a knife just scotch them a cross. Take the heads and mash them, boil them in small beer or ale, with a little whole pepper and an onion. Let it boil a quarter of an hour then strain it; thicken it with butter, salt, flour; add a good deal of mustard. Lay the fish in a dish and pour the sauce into a bason; or plain melted butter and mustard.

To Broil Cod Sounds

You must first lay them in hot water a few minutes; take them out and rub them well with salt, to take off the skin and black dirt, then they will look white; then put them in water and give them a boil. Take them out and flour them well, pepper and salt them, and broil them. When they are enough, lay them in the dish, and pour melted butter and mustard into the dish. Broil them whole.

To Broil Eels

Take a large eel, skin it and make it clean. Open the belly, cut it in four pieces, take the tail end, strip off the flesh, beat it in a mortar, season it with a little beaten mace, a little grated nutmeg, pepper, and salt, a little parsley and thyme, a little lemon-peel, and equal quantity of crumbs of bread, roll it in a little piece of butter; then mix it again with the yolk of an egg, roll it up again, and fill the three pieces of belly with it. Cut the skin off the eel, wrap the pieces in, and sew up the skin. Broil them well, have butter and an anchovy for sauce, with a piece of lemon.

To Spitchcock Eels

You must split a large eel down the back, and joint the bones, cut it in two or three pieces; melt a little butter, put in a little vinegar and salt, let your eel lie in it two or three minutes; then take the pieces up one by one, turn them round with a little fine skewer, roll them in crumbs of bread, and broil them of a fine brown. Let your sauce be plain butter, with the juice of lemon, or anchovy sauce.

To Broil Eggs

First put your salamander into the fire, then cut a slice round a quartern loaf, toast it brown, and butter it, lay it in the dish, and set it before the fire: poach seven eggs, just enough to set the whites, take them out carefully, and lay them on your toast; brown them with the salamander, grate some nutmeg over them, squeeze Seville orange over all. Garnish your dish with orange cut in slices.

Pot rest that sat near the fire and kept a kettle warm.

Chap. V

Of Gravies and Sauces

To Draw Gravy

Cut a piece of beef into thin slices, and fry them brown in a stew-pan, with two or three onions, two or three lean slices of bacon; then pour to it a ladle of strong broth, rubbing the brown from the pan very clean; add to it more strong broth, claret, season it and stew it very well. Strain it off and keep it for use.

To Make White Gravy

Take part of a knuckle of veal, or the worst part of a neck of veal, boil about a pound of this with a quart of water, an onion, some whole pepper, six cloves, a little salt, a bunch of sweet herbs, half a nutmeg sliced; let them boil an hour, then strain it off, and keep it for use.

A Gravy Without Meat

Take a glass of small beer, a glass of water, an onion cut small, some pepper and salt, and a little lemon-peel grated, a clove or two, a spoonful of mushroom liquor, or pickled walnut liquor; put this into a bason, then take a piece of butter, put it in a sauce-pan, and set it on the fire; and let it melt, then dredge some flour, and stir it well till the froth slaks, and it will be brown; put in some sliced onion, then put your mixture to the brown butter, and give it a boil up.

Stew pot.

Gravy for a Turkey

Take a pound of lean beef, cut and hack it, then flour it well, put a piece of butter as big as a hen's egg in a stew-pan; when it is a little brown, then pour in three pints of boiling water, and a bundle of sweet herbs, two or three blades of mace, three or four cloves, twelve whole pepper-corns, a little bit of carrot, a little crust of bread toasted brown; cover it close, and let it boil till there is about a pint or less, then season it with salt, and strain it off.

The peddler's wagon brought a wide variety of items, from needles and pins and indigo dye to the news from the neighboring countryside.

Gravy to Make Mutton Eat Like Venison

Take a woodcock, or snipe, that is stale, (the staler the better) pick it, cut it in two, hack it with a knife; put it into a stew-pan, with as much gravy as you shall want, and let it simmer for half an hour; then strain the gravy for use. This will give the mutton so free a flavor of game, that no one can tell it from venison.

Gravy for a Fowl, When You Have No Meat
Ready

Take the neck, liver, and gizzard, boil them in half a pint of water, with a little piece of bread toasted brown, a little pepper and salt, and a little bit of thyme. Let them boil till there is about a quarter of a pint, then pour in half a glass of red wine, boil it and strain it; then bruise the liver well in, and strain it again; thicken it with a little piece of butter rolled in flour, and it will be good.

To Make a Strong Fish Gravy

Take two or three eels, or any fish you have, skin or scale them, gut them and wash them from grit, cut them into little pieces, put them into a sauce-pan, cover them with water, a little crust of bread toasted brown, a blade or two of mace, some whole pepper, a few sweet herbs, and a little bit of lemon-peel. Let it boil till it is rich and good, then have ready a piece of butter, according to your gravy; if a pint, as big as a walnut. Melt it in the sauce-pan, then shake in a little flour, and toss it about till it is brown, and then strain in the gravy to it. Let it boil a few minutes, and it will be good.

To Make Assence of Ham

Take off the fat of a ham, and cut the lean in slices, beat them well and lay them in the bottom of a stew-pan, with slices of carrots, parsnips, and onions; cover your pan, and set it over a gentle fire; let them stew till they begin to stick, then sprinkle on a little flour, and turn them; then moisten with three or four mushrooms, as many truffles, a whole leak, some parsley, and half a dozen cloves: or instead of a leak, a clove of garlick. Put in some crusts of bread, and let them simmer over the fire for a quarter of an hour; strain it and set it aside for use. Any pork or ham does for this, that is well cured.

To Make a Standing Sauce

Take a quart of claret or white wine, put it in a glazed jar, with the juice of two lemons, five large anchovies, some Jamaica pepper whole, some sliced ginger, some mace, a few cloves, a little lemon peel, horse-radish sliced, some sweet herbs, six shallots, two spoonfuls of capers, and their liquor, put all these in a linnen bag, and put it into the wine; stop it close, and set the vessel in a kettle of hot water for an hour, and keep it in a warm place. A spoonful or two of this liquor is good in any sauce.

To Make Sauce for Roasted Meat

Take an anchovy, wash it very clean, and put to it a glass of red wine, a little strong broth or gravy, some nutmeg, one shallot shred, and the juice of a Seville orange; stew these together a little, and pour it to the gravy that runs from your meat.

To Make Sauce for Savory Pies

Take some gravy, some anchovy, a bunch of sweet herbs, an onion, and a little mushroom liquor; boil it a little and thicken it with burnt butter, then add a little claret, open your pie and put it in. This serves for mutton, lamb, veal or beef pies.

A butter paddle was used to work the butter from one part of a large wooden bowl to another as the buttermilk was washed out with cold water.

To Make Sauce for a Sweet Pie

Take some white wine, a little lemon juice, or verjuice, and some sugar; boil it then beat two eggs, and mix them well together; then open your pie and pour it in. This may be used for veal or lamb pies.

To Make Sauce for Fish Pies

Take claret, white wine and vinegar, oyster liquor, anchovies and drawn butter; when the pies are baked, pour it in with a funnel.

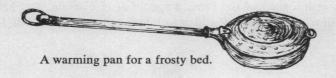

A warming pan for a frosty bed.

To Melt Butter Thick

Your sauce-pan must be well tinned, and very clean. Just moisten the bottom with as small a quantity of water as possible, not above a spoonful to half a pound of butter. You may or may not dust the butter with flour; it is better not to flour it. Cut the butter in slices, and put it into the pan before the little water becomes hot. As it melts, keep the pan shaking one way frequently; And when it is all melted let it boil it up, and it will be smooth, fine, and thick.

To Burn Butter

Put two ounces of butter over a slow fire, in a stew-pan or sauce-pan, without water. When the butter is melted dust on a little flour, and keep it stirring till it grows thick and brown.

To Make Mushroom Sauce for White Fowls Roasted

Take a pint of mushrooms, wash and pick them very clean, and put them into a sauce-pan, with a little salt, some nutmeg, a blade of mace, a pint of cream, and a good piece of butter rolled in flour. Boil these all together, and keep stirring them; then pour your sauce into the dish, and garnish with lemon.

Mushroom Sauce for White Fowls Boiled

Take half a pint of cream, and a quarter of a pound of butter, stir them together one way till it is thick; then add a spoonful of Mushroom Pickle, pickled mushrooms, or such if you have them. Garnish only with lemon.

To Make Cellery Sauce, for Roasted or Baked
Fowls, Turtles, Partridges, or Other Game

Take a large bunch of cellery, wash and pare it very clean, cut it into little thin bits, and boil it softly in a little water till it is tender; then add a little beaten mace, some nutmeg, pepper, and salt, thickened with a good piece of butter rolled in flour; then boil it up and pour it in the dish.

To Make Brown Cellery Sauce

Stew the cellery as above, then add mace, nutmeg, pepper, salt, a piece of butter rolled in flour, with a glass of red wine, a spoonfull of catchup, and half a pint of good gravy: boil all these together, and pour into the dish. Garnish with lemon.

To Make Egg Sauce for Roasted Chicken

Melt your butter thick and fine, chop two or three hard boiled eggs fine, put them into a bason; pour the butter over them, and have good gravy in the dish.

Shallot Sauce for Roasted Fowls

Take five of the shallots peeled and cut small, put them into a sauce-pan, with two spoonfuls of white wine, two of water, and two of vinegar; give them a boil up, and pour them into the dish, with a little pepper and salt. Fowls laid on water cress is very good, without any other sauce.

Shallot Sauce for Scrag of Mutton Boiled

Take two spoonfuls of the liquor the mutton is boiled in, two spoonfuls of vinegar, Two or three shallots cut fine, with a little salt; pour it into a sauce-pan, with a piece of butter as big as a walnut, rolled in a little flour; stir it together, and give it a boil. For those who love shallots, it is the prettiest sauce that can be made to a scrag of mutton.

To Make Lemon Sauce for Boiled Fowls

Take a lemon, pare off the rind, then cut it into slices, and cut it small; take all the kernels out; bruise the liver with two or three spoonfuls of good gravy then melt some butter, mix it all together, give them a boil, and cut in a little lemon-peel very small.

A Pretty Sauce for Boiled Fowls

Take the liver of the fowl, bruise it with a little of the liquor, cut a little lemon-peel fine, add some good butter, and mix the liver by degrees; give it a boil, and pour it into the dish.

To Make Onion Sauce

Boil some large onions in a good deal of water, till they are very tender; put them into a cullender, and when drained, pass them through it with a spoon; put them into a clean sauce-pan, with a good piece of butter, a little salt, and a gill of cream: Stir them over the fire till they are of a good thickness.

To Make Apple Sauce

Take as many boiling apples as you chuse, peel them, and take out all the cores; put them in a sauce-pan with a little water, and a few cloves, and simmer them till quite soft. Then strain off all the water, and beat them up with a little brown sugar and butter.

Bread or Pap Sauce

Take a pint of water, put in a good pint of crumb of bread, a blade of mace, and a little whole pepper; boil it for eight or ten minutes, and then pour the water off; take out the spice, and beat up the bread with a little butter.

Mint Sauce

Take young mint, pick and wash it clean; then shred it fine, put it into a small bason, sprinkle it well with sugar, and pour in vinegar to your palate.

Mint.

Parsley Sauce

Tie the parsley up in a bunch, and boil it till soft; shred it fine, and mix it with melted butter.

To Make Parsley Sauce in Winter, When There Is No Parsley to Be Got

Take a little parsley-seed, tie it up in a clean rag, and boil it for ten minutes in a sauce-pan; then take out the seeds, and let the water cool a little. Take as much of the liquor as you want, drudge in a little flour; and then put in your butter and melt it. Shred a little boiled spinach, and put it in also; and pour it into a boat.

To Make Lobster Sauce

Take a lobster, bruise the body and spawn, that is in the inside, very fine, with the back of a spoon, mince the meat of the tail and claws very small, melt your butter of a good thickness, put in the bruised part, and shake it well together, then put in the minced meat with a little nutmeg grated, and a spoonful of white wine; let it just boil up, and pour it into boats, or over your fish.

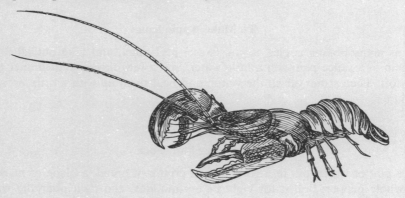

To Make Shrimp Sauce

Put half a pint of shrimps, clean picked, into a gill of good gravy; let it boil up with a lump of butter rolled in flour, and a spoonful of red wine.

To Make Oyster Sauce

Take a pint of oysters that are tolerably large; put them into a sauce-pan with their own liquor, a blade of mace, a little whole pepper, and a bit of lemon-peel; let them stew over the fire till the oysters are plump; pour all into a clean pan, and wash them carefully, one by one, out of the liquor: strain about a gill of the liquor through a fine sieve, add the same quantity of good gravy, cut half a pound of fresh butter in pieces, roll up some in flour, and then put all to your oysters; set it over the fire, shake it round often till it boils, and add a spoonful of white wine; let it just boil, and pour it into your bason or boat.

To Make Anchovy Sauce

Strip an anchovy, bruise it very fine, put it into half a pint of gravy, a quarter of a pound of butter rolled in flour, a spoonful of red wine, and a tea spoonful of catchup: boil all together till it is properly thick, and serve it up.

To Make a Good Fish Sauce

Take half a pint of water, two anchovies split, a clove, a bit of mace, a little lemon-peel, a few peppercorns, and a large spoonful of red wine: boil all together, till your anchovy is disolved, then strain it off, and thicken it with butter rolled in flour. This is the best sauce for skate, maids or thornbacks.

N.B. For other particular sauces, see the receipts for different dishes.

Hanging balance scale.

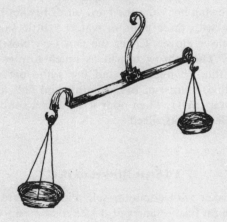

Chap. VI

Of Stewing

To Stew Beef

Take four pounds of stewing beef like the hard fat of brisket beef cut in pieces. Put these into the stew pan with three pints of water; a little salt, pepper, dried marjorum powdered, and three cloves. Cover the pan very close; and let it stew four hours over a slow fire. Then throw into it as much turnips and carrots cut into square pieces, as you think convenient; and the white part of a large leek, two heaps of celery shred fine, a crust of bread burnt, and half a pint of red wine (or good small beer will do as well). Then pour it all into a soup dish, and serve it up hot, garnished with boiled carrots sliced.

To Stew Brisket of Beef

Having rubbed the brisket with common salt and salt-petre, let it lie four days. Then lard the skin with fat bacon, and put it into a stew-pan with a quart of water, a pint of red wine or strong beer, half a pound of butter, a bunch of sweet herbs, three or four shalots, some pepper, and half a nutmeg grated. Cover the pan very close. Stew it over a gentle fire for six hours. Then fry some square pieces of boiled turnips very brown. Strain the liquor the beef was stewed in. Thicken it with burnt butter, and having mixed the turnips with it, pour all together over the beef in a large dish, serve it up hot, and garnish it with lemon sliced. An ox cheek or leg of beef may be served up in the same manner.

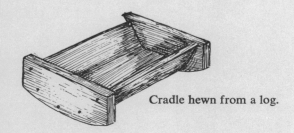

Cradle hewn from a log.

To Stew Beef Gobbets

Cut any piece of beef, except the leg, in pieces, the size of a pullets' egg. Put them in a stew-pan, and cover them with water. Let them stew one hour, and skim them very clean. Then add a sufficient quantity of mace, cloves, and whole pepper tied up loose in a muslin rag, some celery cut small, and salt, turnips, and carrots pared and cut in four, a little parsley, a bundle of sweet herbs, a large crust of bread, and if you please, add an ounce of pearl barley, or rice. Cover all close, and stew it till tender. Then take out the herbs, spices and bread, and add a French roll fried and cut in four. Dish up all together, and send it to table.

Dipping tallow candles.

To Stew Ox Palates

Put the palates into a sauce-pan of cold water, and let them stew very softly over a slow fire till they are tender. Then cut them into pieces, and dish them with cocks-combs and artichoke bottoms cut small; and garnish with lemon sliced, and with sweetbreads stewed for white dishes, and fried for brown ones, and cut also in little pieces.

   N.B. This stew is generally used for improving a fricassee, or ragout of veal, lamb, rabbits, &c.

To Stew Beef Steaks

Half broil the beef steaks; then put them into a stew-pan, season them with pepper and salt according to your palate; just cover them with gravy. Also put in a piece of butter rolled in flour. Let them stew gentle for half an hour, then add the yolks of two eggs beat up, and stir all together for two or three minutes, and serve it up. Garnish with pickles, and horse-radish scraped.

To Stew Beef Collops

Cut raw beef, as veal is cut for Scotch collops. Put the collops into a stew-pan with a little water, a glass of white wine, a shalot, a little dried marjorum rubbed to powder, some salt and pepper, and a slice or two of fat bacon. Set this over a quick fire till the pan be full of gravy, which will be in a little time: add to it a little mushroom juice; and then serve it up hot; and garnish with sliced lemon, or small pickles and red cabbage.

To Stew Veal in General

Let the veal be raw, roasted or boiled; cut into thick slices, and just cover the veal with water in a stew-pan. Season with pepper, salt, and grated nutmeg, a little mace, sweet marjoram, a shallot, and lemon-thyme, or a little grated lemon-peel. Stew all together, and when almost enough, put into the liquor a little good gravy, and mushroom liquor, a glass of white wine, and a little lemon juice. Let these stew a little longer. Then strain off the liquor, and thicken it with butter and flour. Lay the meat in the dish, and pour the sauce over it. Garnish the dish with sippits, and fried oysters, or bits of boiled bacon and sliced lemon, on the rim of the dish.

To Stew a Knuckle of Veal

Boil the knuckle till there is just enough liquor for sauce. To which add one spoonful of catchup, one of red wine, and one of walnut pickle; also some truffles, morels, or dried mushrooms cut small if you please. Boil all together. When enough, take up the meat; lay it in the dish, pour the sauce or liquor over it, and send it to table, garnished with sliced lemon.

To Stew a Neck of Veal

Cut a neck of veal in steaks, and season them well with a mixture of salt, pepper, grated nutmeg, thyme and knotted marjoram. Stew these gently over a slow fire, in cream or new milk, till they be enough. Then add two anchovies, some gravy or strong broth, and a piece of butter rolled in flour. Toss it up till it becomes thick. Then put it in a dish and serve it up hot. Garnish with lemon sliced.

To Stew a Breast of Veal

Let the breast be fat and white, cut off both ends and boil them for gravy. Make a forced meat of the sweet-bread boiled, a few crumbs of bread, a little beef suet, two eggs, pepper and salt, a spoonful or two of cream, and a little grated nutmeg, with which mixture, having raised the thin part of the breast, stuff the veal. Skewer the skin close down, drudge it over with flour; tie it up in a cloth, and boil it in milk and water about an hour.

Barley.

The proper sauce for this dish is made of a little gravy, about a gill of oysters, a few mushrooms sliced fine, and a little juice of lemon, thickened with flour and butter.

To Stew a Pig

Roast a pig till it is thorough hot, then skin it, cut it in pieces, and put it into a stew-pan, with a sufficient quantity of strong gravy, a gill of white wine, some pepper, salt and nutmeg, an onion, a little marjoram, three spoonfuls of elder vinegar, (if you have any) and a piece of butter. Cover all close, and let it stew gently over a slow fire and when enough, serve it up hot, poured upon sippets, and garnished with lemon sliced.

To Stew Mutton Chops

Cut the chops thin, put them into a shallow tin-pan, with a cover that shuts very close. Add a very little water, with a little salt and pepper. Cover the pan very close, and set it over a very slow fire. They will be done in a very few minutes. Dish them up with their own liquor. Garnish with capers, or other pickles.

To Stew a Leg, or Neck of Mutton

Bone the joint to be stewed. Break the bones and put them in a sauce-pan, with a sufficient quantity of whole pepper, salt and mace, to make it relish; also one nutmeg bruised, one anchovy, and one middling turnip; a little faggot of sweet herbs, two middling onions quartered, a pint of ale (and as much red wine, if you like it), two quarts of water, and a hard crust of bread. Stop it close, and let it stew five hours. Then put in the mutton, and let it stew two hours.

To Stew a Hare

Beat it well with a rolling pin in its own blood. Cut it into little bits and fry them. Then put the hare into a stew-pan, with a quart of strong gravy, pepper and salt according to the palate, and let it stew till tender. Thicken it with butter and flour. Serve it up in its gravy, with sippets in the dish, and lemon sliced for garnish.

To Jug a Hare

Having cased the hare, turn the blood out of the body into the jug. Then cut the hare to pieces, but do not wash it. Then cut three quarters of a pound of fat bacon into thin slices. Pour upon the blood about a pint of strong old pale beer: put into the jug a middling sized onion, stuck with three or four cloves, and a bunch of sweet herbs; and having seasoned the hare with pepper, salt, nutmeg, and lemon peel grated, put in the meat, a layer of hare, and a layer of bacon. Then stop the jug close, so that the season be kept in entirely; put the jug into a kettle of water over the fire, and let it stew three hours, then strain off the liquor, and having thickened it with burnt butter, serve it up hot, garnished with lemon sliced.

To Stew a Turkey or Fowl

Take a turkey or fowl, put it into a sauce-pan, or pot, with a sufficient quantity of gravy or good broth; a bunch of cellery, pepper, and allspice, tied loose, with an onion and a sprig of thyme. When these have stewed softly till enough, take up the turkey or fowl; thicken the liquor it was stewed in with butter and flour; and having dished the turkey, or fowl, pour the sauce into the dish.

To Stew Chickens

Cut two chickens into quarters, wash them and put them into a clean sauce-pan, with a pint of water, half a pint of red wine, some mace, pepper, a bundle of sweet herbs, an onion, and a piece of stale crust of bread. Cover them close, and stew them half an hour. Then put in a piece of butter, as big as an egg, rolled in flour, and cover it again close for five or six minutes. Shake the sauce-pan about, and take out the onion and sweet herbs. Garnish with sliced lemon.

N.B. Rabbits, partridges, &c. may be done the same way; and it is the most innocent manner for sick, or lying-in persons.

To Stew Pigeons

Stuff the bellies of the pigeons with a seasoning made of ground pepper, salt, beaten mace, and some sweet herbs shred very fine. Tie up the neck and vent, and when half roasted, put them into a stew pan, with a sufficient quantity of gravy, a little white wine, some pickled mushrooms, and a bit of lemon-peel. Let them stew till enough. Then take them out, thicken the liquor with butter and the yolks of eggs. Dish the pigeons, and pour the sauce over them. Garnish with lemon.

N.B. If you would enrich this receipt—You may, when the pigeons are almost done, put in some artichoke bottoms, boiled and fried in butter, or asparagus tops boiled.

Porringer.

To Jug Pigeons

Truss and season the pigeons with pepper and salt; and having stuffed them with a mixture of their own liver, mixed with beef suet, bread crumbs, parsley, marjoram, and two eggs, sew them up at both ends, and put them into the jug, the breast downwards, with half a pound of butter. Stop up the jug, so as that no steam can get out, then set them into a pot of water to stew. They will take two hours and more in doing, and they must boil all the time. When stewed enough take them out of the gravy, trim off the fat clean; put a spoonful of cream, a little lemon-peel, an anchovy sliced, a few mushrooms, and a little white wine to the gravy, and having thickened it with butter and flour, & dished up the pigeons, pour the sauce over them. Garnish with sliced lemon.

To Stew Ducks

Dress and clean your ducks well, and put them into a stew-pan with strong beef gravy, a glass of red wine, a little whole pepper, an onion, an anchovy, and lemon peel. When well stewed, thicken the gravy with butter an flour, and serve all up together, garnished with parsley.

To Stew Wild Fowl

Half roast a wild duck, &c. Then cut it into bits. When cold, put it into a stew-pan with a sufficient quantity of beef gravy, and let it stew till tender. Then thicken it with burnt butter, and serve it up all together, with sippits within the sides, and lemon sliced on the rim of the dish.

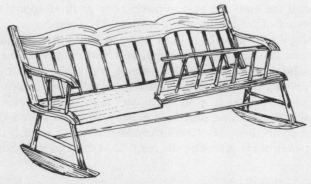

A bench rocker where a mother could sit and safely rock her baby as she did her sewing or other handwork. The cradle rail could be lowered when not in use.

To Stew Giblets

Let the giblets be clean picked and washed, the feet skinned, and the bill cut off, the head split in two, the pinion bones broken, the liver and gizzard cut in four, and the neck in two pieces; put them into half a pint of water with pepper, salt, a small onion, & sweet herbs. Cover the sauce-pan close, and let them stew till enough upon a slow fire. Then season them with salt, take out the onion, and herbs, and pour them into a dish with all the liquor.

Trade sign that identified the maker of boots even to a customer who could not read.

To Stew a Carp or Tench

Scrape them very clean, then gut them, wash them and the roes in a pint of good stale beer, to preserve all the blood and boil the carp with a little salt in the water.

In the mean time strain the beer, and put it into a sauce-pan, with a pint of red wine, two or three blades of mace, some whole pepper, black and white, an onion stuck with cloves, half a nutmeg bruised, a bundle of sweet herbs, a piece of lemon peel as big as a six pence, an anchovy, and a little piece of horse-radish. Let these boil together softly for a quarter of an hour, covered close; then strain the liquor and add to it half the hard roe beat to pieces, two or three spoonfuls of catchup, a quarter of a pound of fresh butter, and a spoonful of mushroom pickle; let it boil, and keep stirring it till the sauce is thick and enough; if it wants any salt, you must put some in; then take the rest of the roe, and beat it up with the yolk of an egg, some nutmeg, and a little lemon-peel cut small; fry it in fresh butter in little cakes, and some pieces of bread cut three-corner ways and fried brown. When the carp are enough take them up, pour your sauce over them, lay the cakes round the dish, with horse-radish scraped fine, and fried parsley. The rest lay on the carp, and put the fried bread about them, lay round them sliced lemon garnish upon the edge of the dish, and two or three pieces on the carp. Send them to table hot.

To Stew a Cod

Cut your cod in slices an inch thick, lay them in the bottom of a large stew-pan season them with nutmeg, beaten pepper, and salt, a bunch of sweet herbs, and an onion, half a pint of white wine, and a quarter of a pint of water; cover it close and let it simmer softly for five or six minutes; then squeeze in the juice of a lemon; put in a few oysters and the liquor, strained, a piece of butter as big as an egg, rolled in flour, and a blade or two of mace; cover it close, and let it stew softly, shaking the pan often. When it is enough, take out the sweet-breads and onion, and dish it up; pour the sauce over it. Garnish with lemon.

To Stew Eels

Skin, gut, and wash them very clean in six or eight waters, to wash away all the sand; then cut them in pieces, about as large as your finger; put just enough water in the pan for sauce, and an onion stuck with cloves, a little bundle of sweet herbs, a blade of mace, and some whole pepper in a thin muslin rag. Cover the pan and let them stew very softly.

Look at them now and then; put in a little piece of butter rolled in flour, and a little chopped parsley. When you find they are quite tender and well done, take out the onion, spice, and sweet herbs. Put in salt enough to season them and dish them up with the sauce.

To Stew Oysters or Muscels

Plump them in their own liquor; then; having drained off the liquor, wash them clean in salt water. Set the liquor drained from the oysters, or so much as necessary, with the addition of an equal quantity of water and white wine, a little whole pepper, and a blade of mace, over the fire, and boil it well. Then put in the oysters, and let them just boil up, and thicken it with a piece of butter and flour; Some will add the yolk of an egg. Serve them up with sippets and the liquor, and garnish the dish with grated bread, or sliced lemon.

To Stew Spinach and Eggs

Pick and wash your spinach very clean, put it into a sauce-pan, with a little salt: cover it close, shake the pan often, when it is just tender, and whilst it is green, throw it into a sieve to drain, and lay it in your dish. In the mean time have a stew-pan of water boiling, break as many eggs in cups as you would poach. When the water boils, put in the eggs, have an egg slice ready to take them out with, and lay them on the spinach, and garnish with orange cut in quarters, and send up melted butter in a cup.

To Stew Parsnips

Boil them tender, scrape them from the dirt, cut them into slices, put them into a sauce-pan with cream enough for sauce, a piece of butter rolled in flour, a little salt, and shake the sauce-pan often. When the cream boils, pour them into a plate for a corner dish, or a side dish at supper.

To Stew Cucumbers

Pare twelve cucumbers, and slice them as thick as a crown piece; put them into a drain, and then lay them in a coarse cloth till they are dry; flour them and fry them brown in butter; pour out the fat, then put to them some gravy, a little claret, some pepper, cloves, and mace, and let them stew a little; then roll a bit of butter in flour, and toss them up; season with salt. You may add a little mushroom liquor.

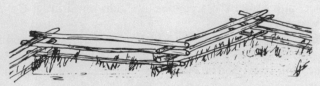

A zigzag split-rail fence.

To Stew Pease and Lettice

Take a quart of green pease, two nice lettices clean washed and picked, cut them small a cross, put all into a sauce-pan, with a quarter of a pound of butter, pepper and salt to your palate; cover them close and let them stew softly, shake the pan often. Let them stew ten minutes, then shake in a little flour, toss them round, and pour in half a pint of good gravy; put in a little bundle of sweet herbs, and an onion, with three cloves, and a blade of mace stuck in it. Cover the pan close, and let them stew a quarter of an hour; then take out the onion and sweet herbs, and pour all into the dish.

To Stew Red Cabbage

Take a red cabbage, lay it in cold water an hour, cut it into thin slices a cross, and them into little pieces. Put it into a stew-pan, with a pound of sausages, a pint of gravy a little bit of ham or lean bacon; cover it close, and let it stew half an hour; then take the pan off the fire, and skim off the fat, shake in a little flour, and set it on again. Let it stew two or three minutes, then lay the sausages in the dish and pour the rest all over. You may, before you take it up, put in half a spoonful of vinegar.

To Stew Pears

Pare six pears, and either quarter them or do them whole as they make a pretty dish with some whole, and the rest cut in quarters, and the cores taken out. Lay them in a deep earthen pot, with a few cloves, a piece of lemon peel, a gill of red wine, and a quarter of a pound of fine sugar. If the pears are very large, they will take half a pound of sugar, and half a pint of red wine; cover them close with brown paper, and bake them till they are enough.

Serve them hot or cold, just as you like them, and they will be very good with water in the place of wine.

"Niddy-noddy, two heads and one body," a hand-held reel used to wind and measure yarn. The "heads" were about eighteen inches apart and once around was equal to two yards of yarn.

To Stew Mushrooms

Take fresh mushrooms, either in buttons, or when the tops are spread, clean them well, washing the buttons with a wet flannel, and the tops must have their skins pulled off, and their gills scraped out, if they happen to be sound, or else do not use them; cut the tops, if they are good, in large pieces, and put them all together in a sauce-pan, without any liquor, cover it close, and let them stew gently, with a little salt, till they are tender, and covered with liquor; then take out your mushrooms, and drain them, or else put some pepper to them, with some white wine, and when they have boiled up, pour off the sauce, and thicken it with a little butter rolled in flour; some will put in a shallot at the first, and other spice, but that will spoil the flavour of the mushrooms, which everybody desires to preserve.

Chap. VII

Of Hashes

To Hash Beef

Take the raw part of any joint of beef; and cut it into thin slices, about the length of a little finger, and about the same breadth. Take also a little water, and an equal quantity of stale beer; boil it well with a large onion cut in two, pepper and salt: then take a piece of butter rolled in flour, and stir it in the pan till it burns. Put it into the sauce and let it boil for a minute or two. Then put in the sliced beef, but you must only just let it warm through. Some add mushrooms or walnut liquor, or catchup. Serve this up to table in a soup-dish, garnished with pickles.

To Hash Mutton

Take mutton half roasted, and cut it in pieces as big as half a crown; then put into the sauce-pan half a pint of claret, as much strong broth or gravy, (or water, if you have not the other) one anchovy, a shallot, a little whole pepper, some nutmeg grated, and salt to your taste; let these stew a little, then put in the meat, and a few capers and samphire shred; when it is hot through, thicken it up with a piece of fresh butter rolled in flour; toast sippets, and lay them in the dish, and pour the meat on them. Garnish with lemon.

To Hash Lamb's Head and Pluck

Boil the head and pluck a quarter of an hour, at most, the heart five minutes, the liver and lights half an hour. Cut the heart, liver and lights into small square bits, not bigger than a pea. Make a gravy of the liquor that runs from the head, and a quarter of a pint of the liquor in which it is boiled, a little walnut liquor or catchup, and a little vinegar, pepper and salt. Then put in the brains, and the hashed meat, shake them well together in the liquor, which should be only just as much as to wet the meat. Pour all upon sippets in a hollow dish; and, having grilled the head before the fire, or with a salamander, lay it open with the brown side upwards, upon the hashed liver, &c. Garnish with sliced pickled cucumbers, and thin slices of bacon broiled.

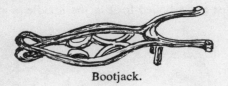

Bootjack.

To Mince Veal

Take any part of the veal that is under done, either roasted or boiled, and shred it as fine as possible with a knife. Then take a sufficient quantity of beef gravy, disolve in it the quantity of a hazel nut of cavear to half a pound of meat, and then put into the gravy the minced veal, and let it boil not above a minute. Pour it into a soup plate or dish upon sippets of bread toasted; and garnish the dish with pickled cucumbers, &c., or with thin slices of bacon broiled.

To Hash a Calf's Head Brown

Take a calf's head and boil it; when it is cold, take one half of the head and cut off the meat in thin slices, put it into a stew-pan, with a little brown gravy, put to it a spoonful or two of walnut pickle, a spoonful of catchup, a little claret, a little shred mace, a few capers shred, or a little mango; boil it over a stove, and thicken it with butter and flour; take the other part of the head, cut off the bone ends, and score it with a knife, season it with a little pepper and salt, rub it over with the yolk of an egg, and strew over a few bread crumbs, and a little parsley; then set it before the fire to broil till it is brown; and when you dish up the other part, lay this in the middle; lay about your hash brain cakes, with forced meat balls, and crisp bacon.

To Make the Brain Cakes

Take a handful of bread crumbs, a little shred lemon peel, pepper, salt, nutmeg, sweet marjoram, parsley shred fine, and the yolks of three eggs; take the brains and skin them, boil and chop them small, so mix them all together; take a little butter in your pan when you fry them, and drop them in as you do fritters, and if they run in your pan, put in a handful more of bread crumbs.

To Hash a Calf's Head White

Take a calf's head, and boil it as much as you would do for eating, when it is cold cut it in thin slices, and put them into a stew-pan, with a white gravy; then put to it a little shred mace, salt, a pint of oysters, a few shred mushrooms, lemon-peel, three spoonfuls of white wine, and some juice of lemon; shake all together, and boil it over the stove, and thicken it up with a little flour and butter. When you put it in your dish, you must put a boiled fowl in the middle, and a few slices of crisp bacon round the dish.

If a cow went through or over fences it could be restrained with a yoke around its neck. A bar was sometimes added, extending out in front from the yoke. This would catch in the fence rails and was commonly called a "cow-poke."

To Dress a Mock Turtle

Take a calf's head, and scald off the hair as you would do off a pig; then clean it, cut off the horny part in thin slices, with as little of the lean as possible; put in the brains and the giblets of a goose well boiled; have ready between a quart and three pints of Madeira wine, a large teaspoonful of Cayan pepper, a large onion cut very small; half the peel of a large lemon shred as fine as possible, a little salt, the juice of two lemons, and sweet herbs cut small; stew all these together, till the meat is very tender, which will be in about an hour and a half; and then have ready the back shell of a turtle, lined with a paste of flour and water, which you must first set in the oven to harden; then put in the ingredients, and set it into the oven to brown the top; and when that is done, suit your garnish at the top with the yolks of eggs boiled hard and forced meat balls.

N.B. If you cannot get the shell of a turtle, a China soup-dish will do as well; and the setting may be omitted.

To Hash Cold Fowl

Cut your fowl up, divide the legs, wings, breast, &c., into two or three pieces; then put them into a stew-pan, with a blade or two of mace, a little flour, and throw in some good gravy; when it begins to simmer, put in a few pickled mushrooms, and a lump of butter rolled in flour. When it boils, give it a toss or two, and pour it into the dish. Garnish with sliced lemon and barberries.

To Hash a Hare

Cut up your hare intirely, put it into a stew-pan with some good gravy, and a gill of red wine, some shred lemon-peel, and a bundle of sweet-herbs; let it stew for an hour; then add some forced meat balls, and yolks of twelve hard-boiled eggs, with truffles and morells. Give them a boil up, then take out the herbs, place the hare handsomely on the dish, and pour the gravy, &c. over it. Garnish with sliced lemon and barberries.

A wooden yoke carved to fit upon the shoulders and used for carrying heavy buckets.

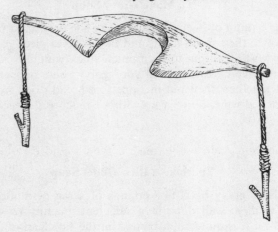

Chap. VIII

Of Soups

To Make Gravy Soup

Take the bones of a rump of beef, and a piece of the neck, and boil it till you have all the goodness of it; then strain it off, and take a good piece of butter, put it in a stew-pan, and brown it, then put to it an onion stuck with cloves, some cellery, endive, spinach, and three carrots; put to your gravy some pepper, salt, and cloves, and let it boil all together; then put in sippets of bread dried by the fire; and you may add a glass of red wine. Serve it up with a French roll toasted, and laid in the middle.

To Make a Rich Giblet Soup

Take four pounds of gravy beef, two pounds of scrag of mutton, two pounds of scrag of veal; stew them well done in a sufficient quantity of water for a strong broth, let it stand till it is quite cold, then skim the fat clean off. Take two pair of giblets well scalded and cleaned, put them into your broth, and let them simmer till they are stewed tender; then take out your giblets, and run the soup through a fine sieve to catch the small bones; then take an ounce of butter, and put it into a stew-pan, mixing a proper quantity of flour, which make it a fine light brown. Take a small handful of chives, the same of parsley, very little pennyroyal, and a very little sweet marjoram; chop all these herbs together excessive small; put your soup over a slow fire, put in your giblets, butter and flour, and small herbs; then take a pint of Madeira wine, some Cayenne pepper, and salt to your palate. Let them all simmer together, till the herbs are tender, and the soup is finished. Send it to table with the giblets in it.

   N.B. The livers must be stewed in a sauce-pan by themselves, and put in the dish when you serve it up.

To Make Good Pease Soup

Take a quart of split pease, put them into a gallon of soft water, with a faggot of herbs, some whole Jamaica and black pepper, two or three onions, a pound of lean beef, a pound of mutton, and a pound of the belly piece of salt pork; boil all together, till your meat is thoroughly tender, and your soup strong; then strain it through a sieve, and put it into a clean sauce-pan; cut and wash three or four large heads of cellery, some spinach, and a handful of dried mint, rubbed fine; boil it till your cellery is tender; then serve it up with toasted bread cut in dice.

A warming shelf that could be placed close to the fire to keep several dishes warm till serving time.

To Make Green Pease Soup

Have a knuckle of veal of four pounds, a pint and a half of the oldest green pease shelled, set them over the fire, with five quarts of water; add two or three blades of mace, a quarter of an ounce of whole pepper, a small onion stuck with three cloves, and a faggot of sweet herbs, cover it close and let it boil till half is wasted; strain it off, pass your liquor through a sieve, put it into a clean sauce-pan, with a pint of the youngest pease, the heart of a cabbage, a lettice or two, and the white part of three or four heads of cellery cut small; cover it close, and let it stew for an hour. If you think it is not thick enough, take some of your soup, and put in half a spoonful of flour; stir it in a bason till it is smooth; pour it into your soup; stir it well together, and let it boil for ten minutes, then dish it up with the crust of a French roll.

To Make White Portable Soup

Take a leg of veal, bone it, and take off all the skin and fat, take likewise two dozen of fowls, or chickens feet washed clean, and chopped to pieces; put all into a large stoving-pot, with three gallons of soft water, and let it stove gently, till the meat is so tender, as to separate. You must keep your pot tight covered, and a constant fire during the time of its stoving; in about seven or eight hours, try your jelly in a cup, and when quite cold, if it is so stiff, you cannot cut it with a knife, take it off, and strain it through a sieve, and take off all the fat and scum first with a spoon, and then with philtering paper. Provide China cups, and fill them with the clear jelly; set them in a gravy-pan or a large stew-pan of boiling water over a stove; in this water boil your jelly in the cups, till it is as thick as glue. After which, let them stand in the water till they are quite cold: Before you turn them out of your cups, run the edge of a knife round them, to loosen them; then turn them upon a piece of new flannel, which will draw out all the moisture gradually. Turn them every six or eight hours, till they are perfectly dry, and like a piece of glue; keep them in as dry a place as you can, and in a little time they will be so dry, that you may carry them in your pocket, without the least inconvenience. When you want to use it, take a piece about the bigness of a walnut, and pour a pint of boiling water on it, stirring it till it is disolved; season it with salt to your taste, and you will have a bason of strong broth. If you want a dish of soup, boil vermicelli in water; then to a cake of your soup, pour a pint of water, so that four cakes will make two quarts; when it is thoroughly melted, set it over the fire just to simmer; pour it into the dish, put in thin slices of bread hardened before the fire, and the vermicelli upon them. Thus you have a dish of soup in about half an hour. Whilst this is doing, you may have any thing drest to follow, which will not only be a good addition to your dinner, but saving time.

Note. You must season it to your palate, as there is no salt, or seasoning of any kind in the preparation.

A dug well with a windlass to raise the oaken bucket.

To Make a Brown Portable Soup

Take a large leg of beef, bone it, and take off the skin, and what fat you can; put it into a stoving-pot with a tight cover; put to it about four gallons of soft water, with six anchovies, half an ounce of mace, a few cloves, half an ounce of whole white pepper, three onions cut in two, a faggot of thyme, sweet marjoram and parsley, with the bottom crust of a two penny loaf that is well hacked, cover it very close and let it have a constant fire to do leisurely for seven or eight hours; then stir it very well together, to make the meat separate. Cover it close again, and in an hour try your broth in a cup, to see if it will glutinate; if it does, take it off, and strain it through a canvas jelly bag into a clean pan; then have China, or well glazed

Mortar and pestle.

earthen cups, and fill them with the clear jelly; put them into a broad gravy-pan, or stew-pan, with boiling water; set in the cups, and let them boil in that till they are perfectly glue. When they are almost cold, run a knife round them, and turn them upon a piece of new flannel, to draw out all the moisture; in six or seven hours turn them, and do so till they are perfectly hard and dry; put them into stone jars, and keep them in a dry place.

This is very good for soups, sauces, or gravies. When you intend to make it into soup, shred and wash very clean what herbs you have to enrich it, as cellery, endive, chervil, leeks, lettice, or indeed what herbs you can get; boil them in water till they are tender, drain them off, and with the water dissolve what quantity of portable soup you please, according to the strength you would have it. If you are where you can get it, fry a French roll, and put in the middle of your dish, moistened first with some of your soup, and when your cakes are thoroughly melted, put your herbs to it, and set it over the fire till it is just at boiling; then dish it up and send it to table.

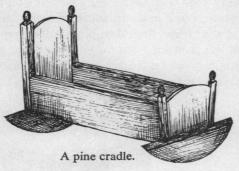

A pine cradle.

To Make Vermicelli Soup

Take two quarts of strong veal broth, put it into a clean sauce-pan, with a piece of bacon stuck with cloves, and half an ounce of butter rolled in flour; then take a small fowl trussed to boil, break the breast bone, and put it into your soup; stove it close, and let it stew three quarters of an hour; take about two ounces of vermicelli, and put to it some of the broth; set it over the fire till it is quite tender. When your soup is ready, take out the fowl, and put it into the dish; take out your bacon, skim your soup as clean as possible; then pour it on the fowl, and lay your vermicelli all over it; Cut some French bread then, put it into your soup, and send it to table.

If you chuse it, you may make your soup with a knuckle of veal, and send a handsome piece of it in the middle of the dish, instead of the fowl.

To Make Soup Lorraine

Have ready a strong veal broth, that is white, & clean scummed from all fat; blanch a pound of almonds, beat them in a mortar with a little water to prevent their oiling, and the yolks of four poached eggs, the lean part of the legs, and all the white part of a roasted fowl; pound all together as fine as possible; then take three quarts of the veal broth put it into a clean stew-pan, put your ingredients in, and mix them well together; Chip in the crust of two French rolls well rasped; boil all together over a stove, or a clear fire. Take a French roll, cut a piece out of the top, and take out all the crumb; mince the white part of a roasted fowl very fine, season it with pepper, salt, nutmeg, and a little beaten mace; put in about an ounce of butter, and moisten it with two spoonfuls of your soup strained to it; set it over the stove to be thorough hot: Cut some French rolls in slices, and set them before the fire to crisp; then strain off your soup through a tammy or a lawn strainer, into another clean stew-pot; let it stew till it is as thick as cream; then have your dish ready; put in some of your crisp bread; fill your roll with the mince, and lay on the top as close as possible; put it in the middle of the dish, and pour a ladleful of your soup over it; put in your bread first, then pour in the soup, till the dish is full. Garnish with petty patties; or make a rim for your dish, and garnish with lemon raced.

If you please, you may send a chicken boned in the middle, instead of the roll; or you may send it to table with only crisp bread.

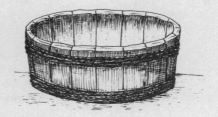

To Make Sorrel Soup with Eggs

Take the chump end of a loin of mutton, and part of a knuckle of veal to make your stock with; season it with pepper, salt, cloves, mace and a faggot of sweet herbs; boil it till it is as rich as you have it; strain it off, and put it into a clean sauce-pan; Put in a young fowl, cover it over, and stove it; then take three or four large handfuls of sorrel washed clean; chop it grosly, fry it in butter, put it to your soup, and let it boil till your fowl is thoroughly done; skim it clean, and send it to table with the fowl in the middle, and fix poached eggs around it. Garnish the dish with fried sippets, and stewed sorrel.

To Make Asparagus Soup

Take five or six pounds of lean beef cut in lumps, and rolled in flour; put it in your stew-pan, with two or three slices of fat bacon at the bottom; then put it over a slow fire, and cover it close, stirring it now and then till the gravy is drawn; then put in two quarts of water, and half a pint of ale. Cover it close, and let it stew gently for an hour, with some whole pepper and salt to your mind; then strain off the liquor, and take off the fat; put in the leaves of white beets, some spinach, some cabbage, lettice, a little mint, some sorrel, and a little sweet marjoram powdered; let these boil up in your liquor, then put in the green tops of asparagus cut small & let them boil till all is tender. Serve it up hot, with a French roll in the middle.

Rich Soups in Lent, or for Fast Days
To Make a Craw Fish Soup

Cleanse them, and boil them in water, salt, and spice; pull off their feet and tails, and fry them; break the rest of them in a stone mortar, season them with savory spices, and an onion, a hard egg, grated bread, and sweet herbs boiled in good strong small beer; strain it, and put to it scaled chopped parsley, and French rolls; then put in the fried craw fish, with a few mushrooms. Garnish the dish with sliced lemon, and the feet and tail of a craw fish.

To Make Oyster Soup

Have ready a good fish stock, then take two quarts of oysters without the beards; bray the hard part in a mortar, with the yolks of ten hard eggs. Set what quantity of fish-stock you shall want over the fire with your oysters; season it with pepper, salt and grated nutmeg. When it boils, put in the eggs, and let it boil till it is as thick as cream. Dish it up with bread cut in dice.

To Make an Eel Soup

Take eels according to the quantity of soup you would make; a pound of eels will make a pint of good soup; to every pound of eels put a quart of water, a crust of bread, two or three blades of mace, a little whole pepper, an onion, and a bundle of sweet herbs; cover them close and let them boil till half of the liquor is wasted; then strain it, toast some bread, and cut it small, lay the bread in the dish, and pour in your soup. If you have a stew-hole, set the dish over it for a minute, and send it to table. If you find your soup not rich enough, you must let it boil till it is as strong as you would have it, and add a piece of carrot to brown it.

To Make a Brown Soup

Into a clean saucepan, put three quarts, or more, of water, with raspings sufficient to thicken it, two or three onions cut across, two or three cloves, some whole pepper, and a little salt; cover it close, and let it boil about an hour and half, then strain it through a sieve; have cellery, carrots, endive, lettice, spinach, and what other herbs you like, not cut too small, and fry them in butter; take a clean stewpan, that is large enough for your ingredients, put in a good piece of butter, dust in flour, and keep it stirring till it is of a fine brown; then pour in your herbs and soup, boil it till the herbs are tender, and the soup of a proper thickness. Have bread cut in dice, and fried brown; pour your soup into the dish, put some of the bread into the soup, the rest in a plate, and serve it up.

To Make a White Soup

Put in a clean sauce-pan, two or three quarts of water, the crumb of a two-penny loaf with a bundle of herbs, some whole pepper, two or three cloves, an onion or two cut across, and a little salt; let it boil covered till it is quite smooth; take cellery, endive and lettice, only the white parts, cut them in pieces, not too small, and boil them until they are very tender. Strain your soup off into a clean stewpan; put your herbs in, with a good piece of butter stirred in till the butter is melted, and let it boil for some time, till it is very smooth. If any scum arises, take it off very clean; Soak a small French roll, nicely rasped, in some of the soup; put in the middle of the dish, pour in your soup, and send it to table.

To Make Onion Soup

First, put a tea-kettle of water on to boil, then slice six Spanish onions, or some of the largest onions you have got; flour them pretty well, then put them into a stewpan that will hold about three quarts, fry them in butter till they are of a fine brown, but not burnt; pour in boiling water sufficient to fill the soup-dish you intent; let it boil, and take half a pound of butter rolled in flour, break it in, and keep it stirring till your butter is melted; As it boils, skim it very well, and put in a little pepper and salt; cut a French roll into slices, and set it before the fire to crisp; poach seven or eight eggs very nicely; cut off all the ragged part of the whites, drain the water from them, and lay them upon every slice of roll; pour your soup into the dish, and put the bread and eggs carefully into the dish with a skimmer. If you have any spinach boiled, lay a leaf between every piece of roll, and send it to table.

If you have any Parmezan cheese, scrape about an ounce very fine, and put it in when you pour on your boiling water; it gives it a very high flavour, and is not to be perceived by the taste what it is.

To Make a Rice Soup

To two quarts of water, put three quarters of a pound of rice, clean picked and washed, with a stick of cinnamon; let it be covered very close, and simmer till your rice is tender; take out the cinnamon, and grate half a nutmeg; beat up the yolk of four eggs, and strain them to half a pint of white wine, and as much pounded sugar as will make it palatable; put this to your soup, and stir it very well together; Set it over the fire, stirring it till it boils, and is of a good thickness; then send it to table.

Basket woven with white oak "splits."

To Make Turnip Soup

Pare a bunch of turnips (save out three or four) put them into a gallon of water, with half an ounce of white pepper, an onion stuck with cloves, three blades of mace, half a nutmeg bruised, a good faggot of sweet herbs, and a large crust of bread. Boil them an hour and a half, then pass them through a sieve; clean a bunch of cellery, cut it small, and put it into your turnips and liquor, with two of the turnips you saved, and two young carrots cut in dice; cover it close and let it stew; then cut turnips and carrots in dice, flour them, and fry them brown in butter, with two large onions cut thin, and fried likewise; put them all into your soup, with some vermicelli; let it boil softly, till your cellery is tender, and your soup is good. Season it with salt to your palate.

To Make Soup Meagre

Take a bunch of cellery washed clean, and cut in pieces, a large handful of spinach, two cabbage lettices, and some parsley; wash all very clean, and shred them small; than take a large clean stew-pan, put in about half a pound of butter, and when it is quite hot, slice four large onions very thin, and put into your butter; stir them well together for two or three minutes; then put in the rest of your herbs; Shake all well together for near twenty minutes; dust in some flour, and stir them together; pour in two quarts of boiling water; season with pepper, salt, and beaten mace: chip a handful of crust of bread, and put in; boil it half an hour, then beat up the yolks of three eggs in a spoonful of vinegar, pour it in, and stir it two or three minutes; then send it to table.

Chap. IX

Of Fricassees

To Fricassee Neat's Tongue

Boil them tender, peel them, cut them into thin slices, and fry them in fresh butter; then pour out the butter; put in as much gravy as will be wanted for sauce, a bundle of sweet herbs, an onion, some pepper and salt, and a blade or two of mace; Simmer all together half an hour. Then take out the tongue, strain the gravy, put it with the tongue in the stew-pan again, beat up the yolks of two eggs, with a glass of white wine, a little grated nutmeg, a piece of butter as big as a walnut rolled in flour; shake all together for four or five minutes, dish it up, and send it to table.

To Fricassee Ox Palates

Put the palates upon the fire in cold water, and let them boil softly till they are very tender; then blance and scrape them clean. Rub them all over with mace, nutmeg, cloves, and pepper beaten fine, and with crumbs of bread. Put them into a stew-pan of hot butter. Fry them brown on both sides. Then, having poured off the fat put as much beef or mutton gravy into the stew-pan as is required for sauce, and an anchovy, a little lemon juice, and salt to make it palatable, and a piece of butter rolled in flour. When these have simmered together a quarter of an hour, dish them up and garnish with sliced lemon.

To Fricassee Tripe

Take the whitest and the thickest seam tripe; cut the white part in thin slices, and put it into a stew-pan, with a little white gravy, a spoonful of white wine, a little lemon juice, and lemon-peel grated. Add to it the yolks of two or three eggs beat very well, with a little thick cream, shred parsley, and two or three chives. Let them all be shook together over a stove or slow fire, till the gravy becomes as thick as cream; but it must not boil, for fear it should curdle. Pour all together into a dish laid with sippets. Garnish with sliced lemon and mushrooms.

To Fricassee a Calf's Head

Take half a calf's head that is boiled tender, cut it into slices, and put it into a stew-pan, with some good veal broth; season it with mace, pepper and salt, an artichoke bottom cut in dice, some force-meat balls first boiled, morels and truffles let these boil together for a quarter of an hour; scum it clean; beat up the yolks of two eggs in a gill of cream, put this in, and shake it round till it is ready to boil; squeeze in a little lemon, and serve it up. Garnish with lemon.

To Fricassee Calf's Feet

Dress the calf's feet, boil them as you would do for eating, take out the long bones, cut them in two, and put them into a stew-pan, with a little white gravy, and a spoonful or two of white wine; take the yolks of two or three eggs, two or three spoonfuls of cream, grate in a little nutmeg and salt, and shake all together with a lump of butter. Garnish your dish with slices of lemon and currants, and serve it up.

Oxen were slow but steady workers in a time when haste was less a part of life. Here they wear a yoke which permitted them to be hitched to a plow or wagon.

To Fricassee Veal Sweetbreads

Cut the sweetbreads in thin slices, the length-way. Dip them in eggs. Season them with pepper, salt, and grated nutmeg. Fry them a light brown. Then put them into a stew-pan, with a sufficient quantity of brown gravy, and a spoonful of lemon-juice; Thicken it with butter and flour. Serve it up altogether, garnished with bits of toasted bacon and crisp parsley.

To Fricassee Lamb Brown

Cut a hind quarter of lamb into thin slices; season them with pepper and salt, a little nutmeg, savory, marjoram, and lemon thyme dried and powdered (some add a shallot.) Then fry it on the fire briskly, and afterwards toss the lamb up in strong gravy, a glass of red wine, a few oysters, some force-meat balls, two palates, a little burnt butter, and an egg or two, or a bit of butter rolled in flour to thicken it. Serve all up in one dish, garnished with sliced lemon.

To Fricassee Lamb White

Take a leg of lamb, half roast it; when it is cold, cut it in slices, put it into a stew-pan with a little white gravy, a shallot shred fine, a little nutmeg, salt, and a few shred capers; let it boil over a stove till the lamb is enough; to thicken your sauce, take three spoonfuls of cream, the yolks of two eggs, a little shred parsley, and beat them well together, then put it into a stew-pan, and shake it till it is thick, but do not let it boil; if this do not make it thick, put in a little flour and butter, to serve it up. Garnish your dish with mushrooms, oysters, and lemon.

To Fricassee Lambstones and Sweetbreads

Have ready some lambstones blanched, parboiled and sliced, and flour two or three sweetbreads; if very thick cut them in two, the yolks of six hard eggs whole; a few pistacho nut kernels, and a few large oysters; fry these all of a fine brown, then pour out all the butter, and add a pint of drawn gravy, the lambstones, some asparagus tops of about an inch long, some grated nutmeg, a little pepper and salt, two shallots shred small and a glass of white wine. Stew all these together for ten minutes, then add the yolks of six eggs beat very fine, with a little white wine, and a little mace; stir all together till it is of a fine thickness, and then dish it up. Garnish with lemon.

To Fricassee Pigs' Ears

Take three or four pig's ears, clean and boil them very tender, cut them in small pieces the length of your finger, and fry them with butter till they be brown; put them into a stew-pan with a little brown gravy, a lump of butter, a spoonful of vinegar, and a little mustard and salt, thickened with flour. Take two or three pig's feet, and boil them very tender, fit for eating; then cut them in two, and take out the large bones; dip them in eggs, and strew with pepper and salt. Then either fry or boil them, and lay them in the middle of the dish with the pigs' ears.

To Fricassee Pig's Pettitoes

Clean the pettitoes very well from hair, etc. Split them in two down the middle. Boil them with the liver, lights and heart, till they are very tender, in half a pint of water or more, according to the quantity of the meat, with an onion, a bunch of sweet herbs, a little whole pepper, and a blade of mace. But in five minutes take out the liver, lights and hearts, mince them very small, grate a little nutmeg over them, and drudge them with flour greatly. And when the pettitoes or feet are quite tender, take them out, strain the liquor in which they were boiled; and then put all together into a sauce pan, with a little salt, a bit of butter as big as a walnut, and either a spoonful of vinegar, or the juice of half a small lemon. Shake the sauce pan often; and after it has simmered five or six minutes, and you have laid some toasted sippets, or slices of bread round the inside of the dish, lay the minced meat and sauce in the middle, and the split pettitoes round it. Garnish with sliced lemon.

To Fricassee a Hare

Boil the hare with apples, onions, and parsley; when it is tender, shred it small, then put thereto a pint of claret, one nutmeg, a little pepper and salt, and two or three anchovies; stir these together, with the yolks of twelve hard eggs shred small; when it is served up, put in as much melted butter as will make it moist; garnish the dish with eggs boiled hard, and cut in halves.

To Fricassee Rabbits White

Halfroast two young rabbits; then skin and cut them in pieces, using only the whitest parts; which you must put into a stew-pan, with a sufficient quantity of white gravy, a small anchovy, a little onion, shred mace, grated lemon-peel and nutmeg; and let it have one boil. Then take a little cream, the yolks of two eggs, a lump of butter, a little piece of lemon and shred parsley, and put them all together into a stew-pan, and shake them over the fire, till they become as white as cream; but do not let the mixture boil, for it will curdle if it does. Garnish the dish with sliced lemon and pickles.

To Fricassee Rabbits Brown

Cut a rabbit's legs in three pieces, and the other parts about the same size. Beat them thin and fry them in butter over a quick fire: when fried put them into a stew-pan with a little gravy a spoonful of catchup and a little grated nutmeg. Shake it up with a little flour and butter, and garnish the dish with fried parsley, made very crisp.

To Fricassee Chickens White

Halfroast the chickens, then having cut them up for eating, skin them, and put them into a stew-pan with a little white gravy, the juice of a lemon, an anchovy for every chicken, and a sufficient quantity of mace and nutmeg grated, and then boil them. Take also the yolks of eggs as much as necessary, a little sweet cream and shred parsley; and put them into a stew-pan with a lump of butter and a little salt. Shake them all the time they are over the fire, but do not let them boil, for that would make them curdle. Serve it up poured upon sippets, and garnish the dish with sliced lemon, or pickled mushrooms.

To Fricassee Chickens Brown

Cut up the chickens raw, in the manner as you do for eating, and flat the pieces a little with a rolling pin. Fry them of a light brown; afterwards put them into a stew-pan, with a sufficient quantity, but not too much gravy, a spoonful or two of white wine to two or three chickens, a little nutmeg and salt. Thicken it up with flour and butter. Garnish with sippets within the dish, and with crisp parsley on the rim.

To Fricassee Pigeons

Quarter each pigeon and fry them. Take also some green pease, and fry them also till they be like to burst. Then pour boiling water upon them, and season the liquid with pepper, salt, onions, garlic, parsley and vinegar. Thicken with yolks of eggs.

To Fricassee Cod

Get the sounds, blanch them, then make them very clean, and cut them into little pieces. If they be dried sounds, you must first boil them tender. Get some of the roes, blanch them and wash them clean, cut them into round pieces about an inch thick, with some of the livers, an equal quantity of each, to make a handsome dish, and a piece of cod of about a pound for the middle. Put them into a stew-pan, season them with a little beaten mace, grated nutmeg and salt, a little sweet herbs, an onion, and a quarter of a pint of fish broth or boiling water; cover them close and let them stew a few minutes; then put in half a pint of red wine, a few oysters with the liquor strained, a piece of butter rolled in flour, shake the pan round, and let them stew softly till they are enough, take out the sweet herbs and onion, and dish it up. Garnish with lemon.

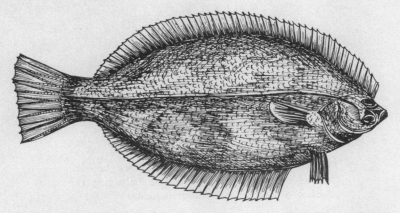

The flounder is born with low-set eyes, but the skull modifies until both are on top.

To Fricassee Soals, Plaice or Flounders

Strip off the black skin of the fish, but not the white, then take out the bones, and cut the flesh into slices about two inches long; dip the slices in the yolks of eggs, and strew over them raspins of bread; then fry them in clarified butter, and when they are fried enough, take them out on a plate and set them by the fire till you have made the following sauce.

Take the bones of the fish, boil them up with water, and put in some anchovy and sweet herbs, such as thyme and parsley, and add a little pepper, cloves and mace. When these have boiled together some time, take the butter in which the fish was fried, put it into a pan over the fire, shake flour into it and keep it stirring while the flour is shaking in; then strain the liquor into it, in which the fish bones, herbs and spice were boiled, and boil it together, till it is very thick, adding lemon juice to your taste. Put your fish into a dish, and pour your sauce over it; serve it up, garnished with slices of lemon and fried parsley.

N.B. This dish may take place on any part of the table, either in the first or second course.

To Fricassee Tench White

Having cleaned your tench very well, cut off their heads, slit them in two, and if large, cut each half in three pieces, if small in two; melt some butter in a stew-pan and put in your tench; dust in some flour, and pour in some boiling water, and a few mushrooms, and season it with salt, pepper, a bundle of sweet herbs, and an onion stuck with cloves. When this boils pour in a pint of white wine boiling hot, let stew till sufficiently wasted; take out the fish, and strain the liquor, saving the mushrooms; bind your fricassee with the yolks of three or four eggs beat up with a little verjuice, some parsley chopped fine, and a little nutmeg grated; stir it all the time it boils, scum it very clean, pour your sauce over the fish, and send it to table.

The small trundle bed could be pushed beneath the larger bed when not in use to help ease the problem of space in the common room.

To Fricassee Tench brown

Prepare your tench as in the other receipt; put some butter and flour into a stew-pan, and brown it; then put in the tench with the same seasoning you did for your white fricassee; when you have tossed them up, moisten them with a little fish broth; boil a pint of white wine, and put to your fricassee, stew it till enough and properly wasted; then take the fish up, and strain the liquor, bind it with a brown cullis, and serve it up. If asparagus or artichokes are in season, you may boil these, and add them to your fricassee.

To Fricassee Eggs White

Boil eight or ten eggs, take off the shells, cut some in halves, and some in quarters, have ready half a pint of cream, a good piece of butter, a little nutmeg, a glass of white wine, and a spoonful of chopped parsley; stir all together over a clear fire till it is thick and smooth; lay your eggs into your dish, and pour the sauce over. Garnish with hard eggs cut in half, oranges quartered, and toasted sippets; send it hot to table.

To Fricassee Eggs Brown

Boil as many eggs hard as you want to fill your dish; take off the shells, and fry them in butter, of a fine brown, pour your fat out of the pan, put in some flour, and a lump of butter, stir it till it is thick, and of a good brown; pour in some boiling water, a gill of Madeira, a little pepper, salt, and beaten mace; boil all together, till it is of a good thickness; scum it and squeeze in a little orange; cut some of your eggs in half, lay the flat side uppermost, and the whole ones between; pour the sauce over. Garnish with fried parsley, and Seville orange cut in small quarters.

To Fricassee Artichoke Bottoms

Take them either dried or pickled; if dried, you lay them in warm water for three or four hours, shifting the water two or three times; then have ready a little cream, and a piece of fresh butter, stirred together one way over the fire till it is melted, then put in the artichokes & when they are hot dish them up.

To Fricassee Mushrooms

Take a quart of fresh mushrooms, make them clean, put them into a sauce-pan, with three spoonfuls of water, and three of milk, and a very little salt, set them on a quick fire, and let them boil up three times; then take them off, grate in a little nutmeg, put in a little beaten mace, half a pint of thick cream, a piece of butter rolled well in flour, put it all together into the sauce-pan, shaking it well all the time. When the liquor is fine and thick, dish them up; be careful they do not curdle. You may stir the sauce-pan carefully with a spoon all the time.

A Betty lamp burned oil and gave out a somewhat smoky light. The last link on the attached chain had a sharp tip which was used to pull the wick up as it burned. It was called a "pickwick."

Chap. X

Of Ragouts

To Ragout a Piece of Beef,
Called Beef a-la-Mode

Take a buttock of beef, interlarded with great lard, rolled up with chopped spice, sage, parsley, thyme and green onions; put it into a great sauce-pan, and bind it close with coarse tape. When it is half done, turn it; let it stand over the fire on a stove twelve hours. It is fit to be eat cold or hot. When it is cold slice it out thin, and toss it up in a fine ragout of sweet breads, oysters, mushrooms and palates.

To Ragout a Breast of Veal

Put a breast of veal, with an onion, a bundle of sweet herbs, a little black pepper and grated nutmeg, a blade or two of mace, and a very little lemon peel grated into a large stew-pan, and just cover it with water; when it grows tender take it up and bone it.

Put the bones into the liquor and boil them till it makes a good gravy. Then strain it off. Add to this liquor a quarter of a pint of rich beef gravy, half an ounce of truffles and morels, a spoonful of catchup, and two spoonfuls of white wine. While these are boiling together, flour the veal and fry it in butter till it becomes to be of a fine brown. Then drain off the butter and pour the gravy to the veal with a few mushrooms.

Boil all together till the liquor becomes rich and thick. Cut the sweetbread into four, and spread the pieces and forced meat balls over the dish; having first laid the veal in the dish, and poured the sauce all over it. Garnish with sliced lemon.

To Ragout a Neck of Veal

Cut it into steaks, flatten them with a rolling-pin, lard them with bacon, and season them with a mixture of salt, pepper, nutmeg grated mace, lemon peel and thyme. Then dip each steak separately in the yolks of eggs. Put all together in a stew-pan, over a slow fire, and keep basting and turning the steaks in order to keep in the gravy. When they are done sufficiently, dish them with half a pint of strong gravy seasoned high, mushrooms and pickles, and forced meat balls dipped in the yolks of eggs. Garnish with stewed and fried oysters.

If you intend a brown ragout, put in a glass of red wine; if a white ragout, put in white wine, with the yolks of eggs beaten up with two or three spoonfuls of cream.

Ox yoke.

To Ragout Veal Sweetbreads

Cut sweetbreads into pieces as big as a walnut; wash and dry them, put them into a stew-pan of hot butter. Stir them till they are brown, and then pour over them as much gravy, mushrooms, pepper, salt, and alspice, as will cover them, and let them stew half an hour. Then pour off the liquor; pass it through a sieve, & thicken it for sauce. Place the veal sweet-breads in the dish, pour the sauce over them, and serve them up, garnished with sliced lemon or orange.

To Ragout a Leg of Mutton

Take off all the fat and skin, and cut the flesh very thin in the right way of the grain. Butter the stew-pan, dust it with flour, and put in the meat, with half a lemon and half an onion cut very small, a blade of mace, and a little bundle of sweet herbs. Stir it a minute or two. Then put in a quarter of a pint of gravy, and an anchovy minced small, mixed with butter and flour. Stir it again for six minutes, and then dish it up.

To Ragout Hog's Feet and Ears

If they are raw or soused, boil the feet and ears till they are tender, after which cut them into thin bits about two inches long, and a quarter of an inch thick. Put them into a stew-pan with half a pint of good gravy, a glass of white wine, a good piece of butter rolled in flour, a little pepper and salt, a good deal of mustard, and half an onion. Stir all together till it becomes of a fine thickness, and then pour it into a dish, meat and gravy together.

To Make a Rich Ragout

Having parboiled lambstones and sweetbreads, and blanched some cocks-combs, cut them all in slices and season them with a mixture of pepper and salt, mace and nutmeg. Then fry them a little in lard: drain them, and toss them up in good gravy, with a bunch of sweet herbs, two shallots, a few mushrooms, truffles and morels. Thicken it with burnt butter, and add a glass of claret or red wine. Garnish the dish with pickled mushrooms, or fried oysters, and sliced lemon.

A Ragout for Made Dishes

Take red wine, gravy and sweet herbs, and spice, in which toss up lambstones, cocks-combs boiled, blanched and sliced with sliced sweetbreads, oysters, mushrooms, truffles and morels; thicken these with brown butter, and use it occasionally when wanted to enrich a ragout of any sort.

Cast-iron stew pot.

A Ragout of Snipes

Take two brace of snipes clean picked; put a piece of butter into a stewpan, and give your snipes a browning; then cut them down the back, and press them flat, but do not take out the trails; put them into a stew-pan with some good gravy, a small glass of red wine, a gill of small mushrooms, and a little beaten mace, and salt. Let them stew five or six minutes; then roll a piece of butter in flour. When it is the thickness of cream, skim it clean and dish them up. Garnish your dish with toasted sippets, and orange cut in small quarters.

A Ragout of Eggs

Boil six eggs hard; then take large mushrooms, peal and scrape them clean, put them into a sauce-pan with a little salt, cover them, and let them boil; put to them a gill of red wine, a good piece of butter rolled in flour, seasoned with mace and nutmeg; let it boil till it is of a good thickness; cut the white of your eggs round, so that you do not breake the yolks; lay some toasted sippets in your dish with the yolks of eggs; then pour over your ragout; garnish your dish with the whites; lay the flat side uppermost and a Seville orange between.

To Ragout Sturgeon

Cut sturgeon into collops, lard, and rub them over with an egg, durst in some flour, and fry them of a fine brown in lard; as soon as they are done, put them into a stew-pan with a pint of good gravy, some sweet herbs shred fine, some slices of lemon, veal sweetbreads cut in pieces, truffles, mushrooms, and a glass of white wine; bind it with a good cullis, till it is of a proper thickness; then take off all the scum very clean; dish it up, and garnish it with barberries and lemon.

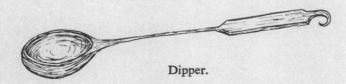

Dipper.

To Ragout Oysters

Open four dozen of the largest Melton oysters, and save the liquor; make a thick batter with cream, the yolks of eggs, nutmeg grated, and parsley chopped fine; Dip the oysters into the batter, and then roll them in bread crumbs and fry them of a fine brown; when they are fried take them up, and lay them on a drainer before the fire; empty your pan, and dust some flour all over it, then put in about two ounces of butter. When it is melted and thick, strain in your oyster liquid, and stir it well together; put in two ounces of Pistacho-nuts shelled, and let them boil; then put in half a pint of white wine, beat up the yolks of two eggs in four spoonfuls of cream; Stir all together till it is of a proper thickness; lay the oysters in the dish, and pour the ragout over. Garnish the dish with a Seville orange cut in small quarters.

Chap. XI

Of Pastry

To Make Paste for Tarts

Take two pounds and a half of butter, to three pounds of flour, and half a pound of fine sugar beaten; rub all your butter in the flour, and make it into a paste with cold milk, and two spoonfuls of brandy.

Puff Paste

Take a quartern of flour, and a pound and a half of butter; rub a third part of the butter in the flour, and make a paste with water; then roll out your paste, and put your butter upon it in bits, and flour it; then fold it up, and roll it again; then put in more butter, and flour it, and fold it up again then put the rest of the butter in, flour it, fold it, and roll it twice before you use it.

Paste for Raised Pies

To half a peck of flour, take two pounds of butter, and put it in pieces in a sauce-pan of water over the fire, and when the butter is melted, make a hole in the flour, skimming off the butter, and put it in the flour, with some of the water; then make it up in a stiff paste, and put it before the fire in a cloth, if you do not use it presently.

Paste for Venison Pasties

Take four pounds of butter to half a peck of flour; rub it all in your flour, but not too small; then make it into paste, and beat it with a rolling pin for an hour before you use it; you may beat three or four eggs, and put into your paste, when you mix it, if you please.

Paste Royal for Patty-pans

Lay down a pound of flour; work it up with half a pound of butter, two ounzes of fine sugar, and four eggs.

Paste for Custards

Lay down flour, and make it into a stiff paste with boiling water; sprinkle it with a little cold water to keep it from cracking.

The raised edge on the lid of the bake kettle held the red-hot coals from the fire, permitting the baking of the top as well as the bottom of its contents.

To Make a Hare Pie

Cut the hare in pieces, break the bones and lay them in the pie; lay on balls, sliced lemon, and butter, and close it with the yolks of hard eggs.

An Umble Pie

Take the humbles of a buck, and boil them, and chop them as small as meat for minced pies, and put to them as much beef suet, eight apples, half a pound of sugar, a pound and a half of currants, a little salt, some mace, cloves, nutmeg, and a little pepper; then mix them together, and put it into a paste; add half a pint of sack, the juice of one lemon and orange, close the pie and when it is baked, serve it up.

A Lumber Pie

Take a pound and a half of fillet of veal, mince it with the same quantity of beef suet, season it with sweet spice, five pippins, a handful of spinach, and a hard lettice, thyme and parsley: Mix with it a penny loaf grated, and the yolks of two or three eggs, sack and orange-flower water, sweet spice, a pound and a half of currants and preserves, and a caudle.

A Shrewsbury Pie

Take a couple of rabbits, cut them in pieces, season them well with pepper and salt, then take some fat pork, and season it in like manner, then take the rabbits livers parboiled, some butter, eggs, pepper and salt, a little sweet marjoram, and a little nutmeg; make these into balls, and lay it in your pie amongst the meat; then take artichoak bottoms, boiled tender, cut in dice, and lay these likewise among the meat, then close your pie, and put in as much white wine and water as you think proper. Bake it and serve it up.

A Lamb Pie

Season the lamb steaks; lay them in the pie with sliced lamb-stones and sweetbreads, savory balls and oysters. Lay on butter, and close the pie with a lear.

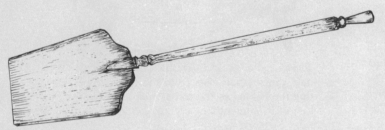

Peel, a long, flat wooden shovel used for reaching into a hot oven.

A Lamb Pie with Currants

Take a leg and a loin of lamb, cut the flesh into small pieces, and season it with a little salt, cloves, mace and nutmeg; then lay the lamb in your paste, and as many currants as you think proper, and some Lisbon sugar, a few raisons stoned and chopped small; add some forced-meat balls, some yolks of hard eggs, with artichoke bottoms, or potatoes that have been boiled and cut in dice, with candied orange and lemon peel cut in slices; put butter on the top, and a little water, then close your pie, bake it gently, and when it is baked take off the top and put in your caudle made of gravy from the bones some white wine and juice of lemon; thicken it with the yolks of two eggs, and a bit of butter. When you pour in your caudle, let it be hot, and shake it well in the pie; then serve it, having laid on the cover.

Note. If you observe too much fat swimming on the liquor of your pie, take it off before you pour on the caudle.

A Mutton Pie

Season the mutton steaks, fill the pie, lay on butter and close it. When it is baked, toss up a handful of chopped capers, cucumbers, and oysters in gravy, with an anchovy and drawn butter.

A Veal Pie

Raise a high, round pie, then cut a fillet of veal into three or four fillets, season it with savory seasoning, and a little minced sage and sweet herbs; lay it in the pie with slices of bacon at the bottom, and between each piece lay on butter and close the pie. When it is baked, and half cold, fill it up with clarified butter.

A Hen Pie

Cut it in pieces, and lay it in the pie; lay on balls, sliced lemon, butter and close it with the yolks of hard eggs, let the lear be thickened with eggs.

A Chicken Pie

Take six small chickens; roll up a piece of butter in sweet herbs; season and lay them into a cover, with the marrow of two bones rolled up in the batter of eggs, a dozen of yolks of eggs boiled hard and two dozen of savory balls; when you serve it up, pour in a quart of good white gravy.

A Sweet Chicken Pie

Break the bones of four chickens, then cut them into small pieces, season them highly with mace, cinnamon and salt; have four yolks of eggs boiled hard and quartered, and five artichoke bottoms, eight ounces of raisons of the sun stoned, eight ounces of preserved citron, lemon and eringo roots, of each alike, eight ounces of marrow, four slices of rined lemon, eight ounces of currents, fifty balls of forced meat, made as for umble pie; put in all, one with the other, but first butter the bottom of the pie, and put in a pound of fresh butter on the top lid, and bake it; then put in a pint of white wine mixed with a little sack, and if you will, the juices of two oranges, sweetening it to your taste. Make it boil, and thicken it with the yolks of two eggs; put it in the pie when both are very hot, and serve it up.

A Turkey Pie

Bone the turkey, season it with savory spice, and lay it in the pie with two capons cut in pieces, to fill up the corners. A goose pie is made the same way, with two rabbits, to fill it up as aforesaid.

A Pigeon Pie

Truss and season the pigeons with savory spices, lard them with bacon, and stuff them with forced meat; lay on lamb-stones, sweet-breads, and butter; close the pie with a lear. A chicken or capon pie may be made the same way.

A Battalia Pie

Take four small chickens, and squab pigeons, four sucking rabbits, cut them in pieces, and season them with savory spice, lay them in the pie, with four sweetbreads sliced, as many sheeps tongues and shivered palates, two pair of lambs stones, twenty or thirty cockscombs, with savoury balls and oysters; lay on butter, and close the pie with a lear.

A Lamb-Stone and Sweet-Bread Pie

Boil, blanch, and slice them, and season them with savory seasoning; lay them in the pie with sliced artichoke bottoms, lay on butter, and close the pie with a lear.

Round wooden village pump.

A Neat's Tongue Pie

Half boil the tongues, blanch them and slice them, season them with savory seasoning, sliced lemon, balls and butter, and then close the pie. When it is baked, take gravy and veal sweet breads, ox palates and cocks-combs, tossed up, and poured into the pie.

A Calf's Head Pie

Almost boil the calf's head, take out the bones, cut it in thin slices, season and mix it with sliced, shivered palates, cocks-combs, oysters, mushrooms and balls. Lay on butter, and close the pie with a lear.

A Venison Pasty

Raise a high round pie, shred a pound of beef suet, and put it into the bottom; cut your venison in pieces and season it with pepper and salt. Lay it on the suet, lay on butter, close the pie and bake it six hours.

An Egg Pie

Shred the yolks of twenty hard eggs with the same quantity of marrow and beef suet; season it with sweet spice, citron, orange and lemon; fill and close the pie.

Minced Pie

Shred a pound of neats tongue parboiled with two pounds of beef suet, five pippins, and a green lemon peel; season it with an ounce of spice, a little salt, a pound of sugar, two pounds of currants, half a pint of sack, a little orange-flower water, the juice of three or four lemons, a quarter of a pound of citron, lemon and orange-peel. Mix these together and fill the pies.

Bed-warming pan.

A Carp Pie

To a quartern of flour put two pounds of butter, rubbing a third part in; then make it into paste with water; then roll in the rest of the butter at three times; lay your paste in the dish, put in some bits of butter on the bottom paste, with pepper and salt; then scale and gut your carps; put them in vinegar, water and salt; then wash them out of the vinegar and water, and dry them, and make the following pudding for the belly of the carp; take the flesh of an eel, and cut it small, put some grated bread, two buttered eggs, an anchovy cut small, a little nutmeg grated, and pepper and salt. Mix these together well, and fill the belly of the carp; then make some force-meat balls of the same mixture; then cut off the tails and fins of the carp, and lay it in the crust with slices of fat bacon, a little mace, and some bits of butter; then close your pie, and before you set it in the oven, pour in half a pint of claret. Serve it hot.

Oyster Pie

Parboil a quart of large oysters in their own liquor, mince them small, and pound them in a mortar, with pistachio nuts, marrow, and sweet herbs, and onion and savory seeds, and a little grated bread; or season as aforesaid whole. Lay on butter and close it.

Flounder Pie

Take twelve large flounders, cut off their tails, fins and heads; then season them with pepper and salt, cloves, mace and nutmeg beaten fine, then take two or three eels well cleaned, and cut in lengths of three inches, and season as before; then lay your flounders and eels in your pie, and the yolks of eight hard eggs, half a pint of pickled mushrooms, an anchovy; a whole onion a bunch of sweet herbs, some lemon-peel grated. You must put three quarters of a pound of butter, on the top, with a quarter of a pint of water, and a gill of white wine, then close your pie and serve it hot, first taking out the onion and bunch of sweet herbs.

Trout Pie

Clean, wash, and scale them, lard them with pieces of silver eel rolled up in spice, and sweet herbs, and bay leaves powdered; lay on and between them the bottoms of sliced artichokes, and mushrooms, oysters, capers, and sliced lemon; lay on butter, and close the pie.

Thread from the spinning wheel was wound on a reel. Forty turns of the reel made a "knot" and twenty knots a skein. The clock reel shown here was made to click after forty turns and, as it was commonly called a "weasel" led to the old song "Pop Goes the Weasel."

Eel Pie

Cut, wash, and season them with sweet seasoning, and a handful of currants; butter, and close it.

Lamprey Pie

Clean, wash, and season them with sweet seasoning; lay them in a coffin with citron and lemon sliced; butter and close the pie.

Artichoke or Potatoe Pie

Take artichoke bottoms, season them with a little mace and cinnamon sliced, eight ounces of candied lemon and citron sliced, eringo roots and prunellas, a slit of each, two ounces of barberries, eight ounces of marrow, eight ounces of raisons of the sun stoned, and two ounces of sugar, butter bottom of the pie, and put in all, one with the other, and eight ounces of butter on the top lid; bake it, and then put on a lear, made as for the chicken Pie.

To Make an Apple or Pear Pie

Make a good puff paste crust, lay some round the sides of the dish, pare and quarter your apples and take out the cores lay a row of apples thick, throw in half the sugar you design for your pie, mince a little lemon-peel fine, throw over and squeeze a little lemon over them, then a few cloves, here and there one, then the rest of your apples and the rest of your sugar. You must sweeten to your palate, and squeeze a little more lemon. Boil the peeling of the apples and the cores in fair water, with a blade of mace, till it is very good; strain it and boil the syrup with a little sugar, till there is but very little and good, pour it into your pie, put on your upper crust and bake it. You may put in a little quince or marmalade if you please.

Thus make a pear pie, but don't put in any quince. You may butter them when they come out of the oven; or beat up the yolks of two eggs and half a pint of cream, with a little nutmeg, sweetened with sugar, take off the lid and pour in the cream. Cut the crust in little three corner pieces, stick about the pie and send it to table.

To Make a Cherry, Plumb or Gooseberry Pie

Make a good crust, lay a little round the sides of your dish, throw sugar at the bottom, and lay in your fruit and sugar at the top. A few red currants does well with them. Put on your lid, and bake it in a slack oven.

Make a plumb pie the same way, and a gooseberry pie. If you would have it red, let it stand a good while in the oven after the bread is drawn. A custard is very good with the gooseberry pie.

To Make Tarts of Divers Kinds

If you propose to make them in patty pans, first butter them well, and then put a thin crust, all over them, in order to your taking them out with the greater ease; but if you make use of either glass or china dishes, add no crust but the top one. Strew a proper quantity of fine sugar at the bottom; and after that lay in your fruit of what sort soever, as you think most proper, and strew a like quantity of the same sugar over them. Then put your lid on, and let them be baked in a slack oven. If you make tarts of apples, pears, apricots, &c, the beaten crust is looked upon as the most proper; but that is submitted to your own particular fancy.

To Make Apple Tarts or Pear Tarts

Pare them first; then cut them into quarters, and take the cores out; in the next place, cut each quarter across again; throw them, so prepared into a sauce-pan, with no more water in it than will just cover the fruit; let them simmer over a slow fire, till they are perfectly tender. Before you set your fruit on the fire, take care to put a good large piece of lemon peel into the water. Have the patty pans in readiness, and strew fine sugar at the bottom; then lay in the fruit, and cover them with as much of the same sugar as you think convenient. Over each tart pour a teaspoonful of lemon juice, and three spoonfuls of the liquor in which they were boiled. Then lay the lid over them, and put them into a slack oven.

If the tarts be made of *apricots* &c, you must neither pare them, nor cut them, nor stone them, nor use lemon juice; which is the only material difference in making them.

Observe, with respect to *preserved tarts,* only lay in the preserved fruit, and put a very thin crust over them, and bake them as short a time as possible.

Orange or Lemon Tarts

Take six large lemons, and rub them very well with salt, and put them in water for two days, with a handful of salt in it; then change them into fresh water every day (without salt) for a fortnight, then boil them for two or three hours till they are tender, cut them into half quarters, and then cut them again three-corner-ways as thin as you can. Take six pippins pared, cored, and quartered, and a pint of fair water; let them boil till the pippins break; put the liquor to your orange or lemon, with half the pulp of the pippens well broken and a pound of sugar. Boil these together a quarter of an hour, then put it in a gallipot and squeeze an orange in it; if it be a lemon tart squeeze a lemon; two spoonfuls is enough for a tart. Your patty will do. Just as your tarts are going into the oven, with a feather, or brush, do them over with melted butter, and then sift doubled refined sugar over them; and this is a pretty icing on them.

Icing for Tarts

Beat and sift a quarter of a pound of fine loaf sugar. Put it into a mortar with the white of one egg, that has been well beat up. Add to these two spoonfuls of rose water, and beat all together till it be so thick as just to run, observing to stir it all one way. It is laid on the tart with a brush or small bunch of feathers dipped in the icing. Set the tarts, when so done, into a cool oven to harden. But take care not to let them stand too long; for that will discolour them.

An Almond Tart, Very Good

To half a pound of almonds blanched, and very finely beat with orange-flower water put a pint of thick cream, two large Naples' biskets grated, and five yolks of eggs with near half a pound of sugar; put all into a dish garnished with a paste, and lay slips in diamonds cross the top; bake it in a cool oven; and when drawn out, stick slips of candied citron in each diamond.

Orange Puffs

Pare off the rinds from *Seville* oranges or lemons, then rub them with salt; let them lie twenty-four hours in water, then boil them in four changes of water, making them first salt; drain them dry, and beat them fine to a paste, then bruise in the pieces of all that you have pared, make it very sweet with fine sugar, and boil it till it is thick. Let it stand till it is cold, and then it will be fit to put in the paste.

Lemon Puffs

Take a pound and a quarter of double refined sugar beaten and sifted, and grate the rinds of two lemons, and mix well with the sugar; then beat the white of two new laid eggs very well, and mix them well with the sugar and lemon peel; beat them together an hour and a quarter, then make them up in what form you please; be quick to set them in a moderate oven; do not take off the papers till cold.

Chap. XII

To make all Sorts of Cakes

A Rich Cake

Take six pounds of the best fresh butter, work it to a cream with your hands; then throw in by degrees three pounds of double refined sugar well beat and sifted: Mix them well together; then work in three pounds of blanched almonds, and having beaten four pounds of eggs, and strained them through a sieve, put them in; beat them altogether till they are thick and look white. Then add half a pint of *French* brandy, half a pint of sack, a small quantity of ginger, about two ounces of mace, cloves, and cinnamon each, and three large nutmegs all beaten in a mortar as fine as possible. Then shake in gradually four pounds of well dried and sifted flour; and when the oven is well prepared, and a thin hoop to bake it in, stir into this mixture (as you put it into the hoop) seven pounds of currants clean washed and rubbed, and such a quantity of candied orange, lemon, and citron in equal proportions, as shall be thought convenient. The oven must be quick, and the cake at least will take four hours to bake it; *Or* you may make two or more cakes out of these ingredients, you must beat it with your hands, and the currants must be dried before the fire, and put into the cake warm.

Another

To a quartern and half of fine flour add six pounds of currants, an ounce of cloves and mace, a little cinnamon, two grated nutmegs, a pound of the best sugar, some candied lemon, orange and citron, cut in thin pieces; a pint of sweet wine; a little orange flower or rose water, a pint of yeast; a quart of cream; two pounds of butter melted, and poured into the middle of the flour. Then strew some flour over the butter and let it stand half an hour before the fire, after which knead it well together and lay it before the fire to make it rise, and work it up very well. Put this mixture into a tin hoop, and bake it two hours and a half in a gentle oven.

A Spanish Cake

Take twelve eggs, three quarters of a pound of the best moist sugar, mill them in a chocolate mill, till they are all of a lather; then mix in one pound of flour, half a pound of pounded almonds, two ounces of candied orange peel, two ounces of citron, four large spoonfuls of orange or rose water, half an ounce of cinnamon, and a glass of sack. It is better when baked in a slow oven.

Portugal Cakes

Put a pound of fine sugar, a pound of fresh butter, five eggs, and a little mace, beaten, into a broad pan; beat it with your hands till it is very light, and looks curdling; then put thereto a pound of flour, half a pound of currants very dry, beat them together, fill tin pans, and bake them in a slack oven. You may make seed-cakes the same way, only put in carraway-seeds instead of currants.

Dutch Cakes

Take five pounds of flour, two ounces of carraway seeds, half a pound of sugar, and something more than a pint of milk, and put into it three quarters of a pound of butter; then make a hole in the middle of the flour, and put in a full pint of good ale-yeast; then pour in the butter and milk, and make these into a paste, letting it stand a quarter of an hour before the fire to rise; then mould it, and roll it into cakes pretty thin; prick them all over pretty much, or they will blister; bake them a quarter of an hour.

Shrewsbury Cakes

Take to one pound of sugar, three pounds of the finest flour, a nutmeg grated, and some beaten cinnamon; the sugar and spice must be sifted into the flour; and wet it with three eggs, and as much melted butter as will make it of a good thickness to roll into a paste; mould it well, and roll it; cut it into what shape you please; perfume them, and prick them before they go into the oven.

Marlborough Cakes

Take eight eggs, yolks and whites, beat and strain them, and put to them a pound of sugar beaten and sifted; beat it three quarters of an hour together, then put in three quarters of a pound of flour well dried, and two ounces of carraway seeds; beat it all well together, and bake it in a quick oven in broad tin pans.

Queen Cakes

Take a pound of sugar, and beat it fine, pour in yolks and two whites of eggs, half a pound of butter, a little rose water, six spoonfuls of warm cream, a pound of currants, and as much flour as will make it up; stir them well together, and put them into your patty pans, being well buttered; bake them in an oven; almost as hot as for manchet for half an hour; then take them out and glaze them, and let them stand but a little after the glazing is on, to rise.

Sugaring off.

Uxbridge Cakes

Take a pound of wheat flour, seven pounds of currants, half a nutmeg, four pounds of butter, rub your butter cold very well amongst the meal. Dress the currants very well in the flour, butter and seasoning, and knead it with so much good new yeast as will make it into a pretty high paste: usually two penny-worth of yeast to that quantity. After it is kneaded well together, let it stand an hour to rise. You may put half a pound of paste in a cake.

A Pound Cake

Take a pound of butter, beat it in an earthen pan with your hand one way till it like a fine thick cream; then have ready twelve eggs, with half the whites; beat them well, and beat them up with the butter, and work into it a pound of flour, a pound of sugar, and a few carraways, well together for an hour with your hand, or a great wooden spoon. Butter a pan and put it in, and then bake it an hour in a quick oven.

A Seed Cake

Take three pounds of fine flour, and two pounds of butter, rub in the flour eight eggs and four whites, a little cream and five spoonfuls of yeast. Mix all together; and put it before the fire to rise; then put in three quarters of a pound of carraway-seeds, and put it in a hoop or tin rim well buttered. An hour and a half will bake it.

Fine Almond Cakes

Take a pound of Jordan almonds, blanch them, beat them very fine with a little orange-flower water, to keep them from oiling; then take a pound and a quarter of fine sugar, boil it to a high candy; then put in your almonds. Then take two fresh lemons, grate off the rind very thin and put as much juice as to make it of a quick taste; then put this mixture into glasses, and set in a stove, stiring often, that it may not candy: so when it is a little dry, part it into little cakes upon sheets of paper or tin to dry.

Saffron Cakes

Take half a peck of the finest flour, a pound of butter, and a pint of cream, or good milk; set the milk on the fire, put in the butter, and a good deal of sugar; then strain saffron to your taste and liking into the milk; take seven or eight eggs, with two yolks, and seven or eight spoonfuls of yeast; then put the milk to it when it is almost cold, with salt and coriander seeds; knead them all together, make them up in reasonable sized cakes, and bake them in a quick oven.

Bootjack.

Orange Cakes

Take the peels of four oranges, being first pared, and the meat taken out; boil them tender, and beat them small in a marble mortar; then take the meat of them, and two or more oranges, the seeds and skins being picked out, and mix it with the peelings that are beaten, set them on the fire, with a spoonful or two of orange-flower water, keeping it stirring till that moisture be pretty well dried up; then have ready, to every pound of that pulp, four pounds and a quarter of double-refined sugar, finely sifted. Make the sugar very hot, and dry it upon the fire, and then mix it and the pulp together, and set it on the fire again, till the sugar be very well melted, but take care it does not boil. You may put in a little peel, small shred or grated; and when it is cold, draw it up in double papers; dry them before the fire, and when you turn them, put two together; or you may keep them in deep glasses or pots, and dry them as you have occasion.

Common Biscuits

Beat up six eggs, with a spoonful of rose water and a spoonful of sack, then add a pound of fine powdered sugar, and a pound of flour; mix them into the eggs by degrees, with an ounce of coriander seeds; mix all well together, shape them on white thin paper or tin moulds, in any form you please. Beat the white of an egg, and with a feather rub them over, and dust fine sugar over them. Set them in an oven moderately heated, till they rise and come to a good colour; and if you have no stove to dry them in, put them into the oven at night, and let them stand till morning.

To Make Wigs

Take three pounds and a half of flour, and three quarters of a pound of butter, and rub it into the flour till none of it be seen; then take a pint or more of new milk, and make it very warm, and a half a pint of new ale-yeast, then make it into a light paste; put in carraway-seeds, and what spice you please; then make it up and lay it before the fire to rise; then work in three quarters of a pound of sugar, and then roll them into what form you please, pretty thin, and put them on tin plates, and hold them before the fire to rise again, before you set them in; your oven must be pretty quick.

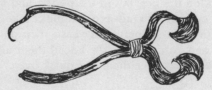

Sugar was purchased in hard loaves that had to be broken to be used. This strange-looking tool is a sugar nipper.

To Make Buns

Take two pounds of fine flour, a pint of ale yeast, put a little sack in the yeast and three eggs beaten; knead all these together with a little warm milk, a little nutmeg, and a little salt. Then lay it before the fire till it rise very light. Then knead in it a pound of fresh butter, and a pound of round carraway-comfits, and bake them in a quick oven on floured papers in what shape you please.

Maccaroons

Take a pound of almonds, let them be scalded, blanched, and thrown into cold water, then dry them in a cloth and pound them in a mortar; moisten them with orange-flower water, or the white of an egg, lest they turn to an oil; after, take an equal quantity of fine powdered sugar with three or four whites of eggs and a little musk; beat them all well together, and shape them on wafer paper with a spoon. Bake them on tin plates in a gentle oven.

Good Fritters

Mix half a pint of good cream, very thick with flour, beat six eggs, leaving out four whites, and to the eggs put six spoonfuls of sack, and strain them into the batter; put in a little grated nutmeg, ginger and cinnamon, all very fine, also a little salt; then put in another half pint of cream, and beat the batter near an hour; pare and slice your apples thin, dip every piece in the batter, and throw them into a pan full of boiling lard.

Pan Cakes

Take a pint of thick cream, six spoonfuls of sack, and half a pint of flour, six eggs (but only three whites) one grated nutmeg, a quarter of a pound of melted butter, a very little salt, and some sugar; fry these thin in a dry pan.

Bread trough in which the dough could lie while rising.

Cheesecakes After the Best Manner

First warm a pint of cream, and then add to it five quarts of milk that is warm from the cow; and when you have put a sufficient quantity of rennet to it, stir it about till it comes to a curd; then put the curd into a cloth, or linen bag, and let the whey be very well drained from it; but take care not to squeeze it hard; when it is sufficiently dry, throw it into a mortar, and beat it till it is as fine as butter. To the curd thus prepared, add half a pound of sweet almonds blanched, and the same quantity of macaroons, both beaten together as fine as powder. If you have none of the last near at hand, make use of Naples biscuits in their stead; then add to your ingredients the yolks of nine eggs that have been well beaten, a whole nutmeg, and half a pound of double refined sugar. When you have mingled all these well together, melt a pound and a quarter of the best fresh butter, and stir it well into it.

As to your puff-paste for your cheesecakes, it must be made in the manner following.

Wet a pound of fine flour with cold water, and then roll it out; put in gradually at least two pounds of the best fresh butter, and shake a small quantity of flour upon each coat as you roll it. Make it just as you use it.

N.B. Some will add to these, both currants and perfumed plumbs.

Cheesecakes Without Rennet

Take a quart of thick cream, and set it over a clear fire, with some quartered nutmegs in it; just as it boils up, put in twelve eggs well beaten; stir it a little while on the fire, till it begins to curdle; then take it off, and gather the curd as for cheese; put it in a clean cloth, tie it together, and hang it up, that the whey may run from it; when it is pretty dry, put it in a stone mortar, with a pound of butter, a quarter of a pint of thick cream, some sack, orange-flour water, and half a pound of fine sugar; then beat and grind all these together for an hour or more, till it is very fine; then pass it through a hair sieve, and fill your patty-pans but half full; you may put currants in half the quantity if you please; a little more than a quarter of an hour will bake them; take the nutmeg out of the cream when it is boiled.

Long-handled waffle iron.

Potatoe or Lemon Cheesecakes

Take six ounces of potatoes, four ounces of lemon-peel, four ounces of sugar, four ounces of butter; boil the lemon-peel tender, pare and scrape the potatoes, boil them tender, and bruise them; beat the lemon-peel with sugar, then beat all together very well, and melt the butter in a little thick cream; mix all together very well, and let it lie till cold; put crust in your patty-pans, and fill them little more than half full. Bake them in a quick oven half an hour; sift some double refined sugar on them as they go into the oven; this quantity will make a dozen small patty-pans.

Chap. XIII

Of Puddings, &c.

To Make a Plain Boiled Pudding

Take a pint of new milk, mix with it six eggs well beaten, two spoonfuls of flour, half a nutmeg grated, a little salt and sugar. Put this mixture into a cloth or bag. Put it into boiling water: and half an hour will boil it. Serve it up with melted butter.

A Light Pudding

Take a pint of cream or new milk from the cow; in which boil a little nutmeg, cinnamon and mace. Take out the spice, and beat up the yolks of eight eggs, and the whites of four, with a glass of sweet mountain wine; to which add a little salt and sugar, and then mix them with the milk, into which put a halfpenny roll, a spoonful of flour, and a little rose water; and having beat them well together, tie all up in a thick cloth, and boil it for an hour. Melt butter, sugar, and a little white wine for sauce, and pour it over the pudding, when dished.

A Quaking Pudding

Take a penny white loaf grated, two spoonfuls of flour of rice, and seven eggs beaten up. Put them in a quart of cream or new milk. Season them with nutmeg grated and white-rose water. Tie it up. Boil it an hour, and then serve it up with plain butter melted, and with sugar and a little wine.

A Fine Biscuit Pudding

Grate three Naples biscuit. Pour a pint of cream or milk over it hot. Cover it close till it be cold. Then add a little grated nutmeg, the yolks of four eggs and two whites beaten, a little orange-flower or rose water, two ounces of powdered sugar, and half a spoonful of flour. Mix these well and boil them in a china bason tied in a cloth, one hour. Turn it out of the bason, and serve it up in a dish with butter, wine, and sugar melted and poured over it.

Puddings could be large or small, boiled or steamed, made of either meat or vegetable or a combination of the two.

Boiled Plumb Puddings

Shred a pound of beef suet very fine, to which add three quarters of a pound of raisons stoned, a little grated nutmeg, a large spoonful of sugar, a little salt, some white wine, four eggs beaten, three spoonfuls of cream, and five spoonfuls of flour. Mix them well, and boil them in a cloth three hours. Pour over this pudding melted butter, when dished.

The Tunbridge Puddings

Pick and dry a pint of great oatmeal. Bruise it, but not small, in a mortar. Boil it a quarter of an hour in new milk. Then cover it close, and let it stand till it be cold. To this, when cold, add eight eggs beaten and strained, a penny loaf grated, half a pound of beef suet shred small, half a nutmeg grated, three spoonfuls of *Madeira* or sack, a quarter of a pound or more of sugar. Mix these well together. Tie it up in a cloth, and boil it three hours. Serve it up with a good deal of butter poured over it.

A Custard Pudding

Take two spoonfuls of fine flour, half a grated nutmeg, a little salt and sugar, six eggs well beaten, and mix them all in a pint of cream or new milk. Boil it in a cloth half an hour; and serve it up with plain butter melted.

A Hunting Pudding

Mix a pound of beef suet shred fine with a pound of fine flour, three quarters of a pound of currants well cleaned, a quarter of a pound of raisons stoned and shred, five eggs, a little grated lemon peel, two spoonfuls of sugar, and a little brandy. Mix them well together. Tie it up in a cloth; and boil it full two hours. Serve it up with white wine and butter melted.

A Boiled Suet Pudding

Take a quart of milk, a pound of suet shred small, four eggs, two spoonfuls of grated ginger, or one of beaten pepper, a teaspoonful of salt. Mix the seasoning and suet first in one pint of the milk, and make a thick batter with flour. Then mix in the rest of the milk with the seasoning and suet, till it becomes a pretty thick batter. Boil it two hours. Serve it with plain butter.

A Steak Pudding

Make a rich crust of a quartern of flour and two pounds of suet shred fine, mixed up with cold water; seasoned with a little salt, and made stiff. The steaks may be either beef or mutton; well seasoned with pepper and salt. Roll the paste out half an inch thick. Lay the steaks upon it, and roll them up in it. Then tie it in a cloth, and put it into boiling water. A small pudding will be done enough in three hours. A large one takes five hours boiling.

N.B. Pigeons eat well this way.

A Boiled Potatoe Pudding

Boil two pounds of potatoes, and beat them in a mortar fine, beat in half a pound of melted butter, boil it half an hour. Pour melted butter over it, with a glass of white wine, or the juice of a Seville orange, and throw sugar all over the pudding and dish.

A Boiled Almond Pudding

Beat a pound of sweet almonds as small as possible, with three spoonfuls of rose-water, and a gill of sack or white wine, and mix in half a pound of fresh butter melted, with five yolks of eggs and two whites, a quart of cream, a quarter of a pound of sugar, half a nutmeg grated, one spoonful of flour, and three spoonfuls of crumbs of white bread; Mix all well together and boil it. It will take half an hour boiling.

A Boiled Rice Pudding

Take a quarter of a pound of rice, and half a pound of raisons stoned. Tie them in a cloth, so as to give the rice room to swell. Boil it two hours. And serve it up with melted butter, sugar, and grated nutmeg thrown over it.

A Prune or Damson Pudding

Take a quart of milk, beat six eggs, half the whites, with half a pint of milk and four spoonfuls of flour, a little salt and two spoonfuls of beaten ginger; then by degrees mix in all the milk, and pound of *prunes*. Tie it in a cloth; boil it an hour, melt butter and pour over it. *Damsons* eat well this way.

An Apple Pudding

Make a good puff paste, roll it out half an inch thick, pare the apples, and core them, enough to fill the crust and close it up. Tie it in a cloth and boil it. If a small pudding two hours; if a large one three or four hours. When it is enough turn it into a dish; cut a piece of crust out of the top, butter and sugar it to the palate; lay on the crust again, and send it to table hot.

N.B. A *pear pudding* and a *damson pudding,* or any sort of *plumbs, apricots, cherries,* or *mulberries,* may be made the same way.

A Plain Baked Pudding

Boil a quart of milk; then stir in flour till thick. Add half a pound of butter, six ounces of sugar, a nutmeg grated, a little salt, ten eggs, but all the whites. Mix them well. Put into a dish buttered, and it will be baked in three quarters of an hour.

A Bread Pudding Baked

Take a pint of cream and a quarter of a pound of butter, set it on the fire, and keep it stirring. When the butter shall be melted, put in as much grated stale bread as will make it pretty light, a nutmeg, a sufficient quantity of sugar, three or four eggs and a little salt. Mix all together. Butter a dish, put it in, and bake it half an hour.

A Millet Pudding

Take half a pound of millet and boil it over night in two quarts of milk. In the morning add six ounces of sugar, six of melted butter, seven eggs, half a nutmeg, a pint of cream, and sweeten it to your taste. Add ten eggs, and half the whites. Bake it.

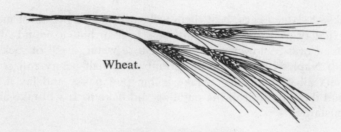

Wheat.

A Marrow Pudding

Boil a quart of cream. Take it off the fire boiling, and slice into it a penny white loaf. Add to it eight ounces of blanched almonds beaten fine, two spoonfuls of white rose-water, the yolk of six eggs, a glass of sack, a little salt, six ounces of candied lemon and citron sliced thin, and half a pound of currants. Mix all together, and put it into a dish rubbed with butter. Half an hour will bake it; and when enough, dust on fine sugar, and serve it up hot.

A Rice Pudding

Beat half a pound of rice to powder. Set it with three pints of new milk upon the fire and let it boil well, and when it grows almost cold, put to it eight eggs well beaten, and half a pound of suet or butter, half a pound of sugar, and a sufficient quantity of cinnamon, nutmeg and mace. Half an hour will bake it.

You may add a few currants and candied lemon and citron peel, or other sweetmeats; and lay a puff paste first all over the sides and rim of the dish.

A Poor Man's Pudding

Take some stale bread; pour over it some hot water, till it is well soaked; then press out the water and wash the bread; add some powdered ginger, nutmeg grated, and a little salt; some rose water or sack, some Lisbon sugar, and some currants; Mix them well together, and lay it in a pan well buttered on the sides; and when it is well flatted with a spoon, lay some pieces of butter on the top; bake it in a gentle oven, and serve it hot. You may turn it out of the pan when it is cold, and it will eat like a fine cheesecake.

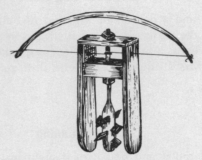

An early egg beater.

An Orange Pudding

Take the yolks of sixteen eggs, beat them well, with half a pound of melted butter, grate in the rind of two fine Seville oranges, beat in half a pound of fine sugar, two spoonfuls of orange-flower water, two of rose water, a gill of sack, half a pint of cream, two Naples biscuits, or the crumb of a half-penny roll soaked in the cream, and mix all well together. Make a thin puff paste, and lay it all over the dish and round the rim, pour in the pudding and bake it. It will take about as long baking as a custard.

A Carrot Pudding

You must take a raw carrot, scrape it very clean and grate it. Take half a pound of the grated carrot, and a pound of grated bread, beat up eight eggs, leave out half the whites, and mix the eggs with half a pint of cream; then stir in the bread and carrot, half a pound of fresh butter melted, half a pint of sack, three spoonfuls of orange-flower water and nutmeg grated. Sweeten to your palate. Mix all well together, and if it is not thin enough, stir in a little new milk or cream. Let it be of moderate thickness: Lay a puff paste all over the dish and pour in the ingredients. Bake it, which will take an hour. It may also be boiled. If so, serve it up with melted butter, and put in white wine and sugar.

Binding grain into a sheaf.

A Quince, Apricot, or White Pear-Plumb Pudding

Scald your quinces very tender, pare them very thin, scrape off the soft; mix it with sugar very sweet, put in a little ginger and a little cinnamon. To a pint of cream you must put three or four yolks of eggs, and stir it into your quinces till they are of a good thickness. It must be pretty thick. So you may do apricots or white pear plumbs, but never pare them. Butter your dish, pour it in, and bake it.

An Italian Pudding

Lay puff paste at the bottom and round the edges of the dish. Upon which pour a mixture of a pint of cream, French rolls enough to thicken it, ten eggs beaten very fine, a nutmeg grated, twelve pippins sliced, some orange peel and sugar, and half a pint of red wine. Half an hour will bake it.

An Apple Pudding

Scald three or four codlins and bruse them through a sieve. Add a quarter of a pound of bisket, a little nutmeg, a pint of cream, ten eggs, but only half the whites. Sweeten to your taste, and bake it.

A Norfolk Dumpling

Make a batter as for pancakes, with a pint of milk, two eggs, a little salt, and as much flour as is needful. Drop this batter, in pieces, into a pan of boiling water. And if the water boils fast, they will be enough in three minutes. Throw them into a sieve or cullendar to drain. Then lay them in a dish. Stir a slice of fresh butter into each, and eat them hot.

A Hard Dumpling

Mix flour and water, and a little salt, like a paste. Roll it into balls, as big as a turkey's egg. Have a pan of boiling water ready. Throw the balls of paste into the water, having first rolled them in flour. They eat best boiled in a beef-pot; and a few currants added make a pretty change. Eat them with butter as above.

Apple Dumplings

Pare and core as many *codlins* as you intend to make dumplings. Make a little cold butter paste. Roll it to the thickness of one's finger; and lap it round every apple singly, and if they be boiled singly in pieces of cloth, so much the better. Put them into boiling water, and they will be enough in half an hour. Serve them up with melted butter and white wine; and garnish with grated sugar about the dish.

Chap. XIV

Of Syllabubs,
Creams, and Flummery

To Make a Fine Syllabub from the Cow

Sweeten a quart of cyder, with double refined sugar, and grate a nutmeg into it; then milk the cow into your liquor. When you have thus added what quantity of milk you think proper, pour half a pint, or more (in proportion to the quantity of syllabub you make) of the sweetest cream you can get all over it.

A Whipt Syllabub

Take two porringers of cream, and one of white wine, grate in the skin of a lemon, take the whites of three eggs, sweeten it to your taste, then whip it with a whisk, take off the froth as it rises, and put it into your syllabub glasses or pots, and they are fit for use.

To Make a Fine Cream

Take a pint of cream, sweeten it to your palate; grate a little nutmeg, put in a spoonful of orange-flower water, and rose water, and two spoonfuls of sack: beat up four eggs and two whites, stir it all together one way over the fire, till it is thick; have cups ready, and pour it in.

Lemon Cream

Take the juice of four large lemons, half a pint of water, a pound of double refined sugar beaten fine, the whites of seven eggs, and the yolk of one beaten very well; mix all together, strain it, set it on a gentle fire, stirring it all the while, and skim it clean; put into it the peel of one lemon when it is very hot; but not to boil; take out the lemon-peel, and pour it into china dishes.

Rasberry Cream

Take a quart of thick sweet cream, and boil it two or three wallops; then take it off the fire, and strain some juice of rasberries into it to your taste; stir it a good while before you put your juice in, that it may be almost cold when you put it to it, and afterwards stir it one way for almost a quarter of an hour; then sweeten it to your taste, and when it is cold you may send it up.

Whipped Cream

Take a quart of thick cream, & the whites of eight eggs beaten with half a pint of sack; mix it together, and sweeten it to your taste with double refined sugar; you may perfume it (if you please) with musk or amber-grease tied in a rag, and steeped a little in the cream; Whip it with a whisk, and a bit of lemon-peel tied in the middle of the whisk. Take off the froth with a spoon, and lay it in your glasses or basons.

To Make a Trifle

Cover the bottom of a dish or bowl with Naples biscuits broke in pieces, macaroons broke in halves, and ratafia cakes. Just wet them all through with sack; then make a good boiled custard, not too thick, and when cold pour it over it, then put a syllabub over that. You may garnish it with ratafia cakes, currant jelly, and flowers.

Flummery

Take a large calf's foot, cut out the great bones, and boil them in two quarts of water; then strain it off, and put to the clear jelly half a pint of thick cream, two ounces of sweet almonds, and an ounce of bitter almonds, well beaten together. Let it just boil, and then strain it off, and when it is as cold as milk from the cow, put it into cups or glasses.

Oatmeal Flummery

Put oatmeal (as much as you want) into a broad deep pan. Then cover it with water, stir it together, and let it stand twelve hours. Then pour off that water clear, and put on a good deal of fresh water, shift it again in twelve hours, and so on in twelve more. Then pour off that water clear, and strain the oatmeal through a coarse hair-sieve, and pour it into a sauce pan keeping it stirring all the time with a stick till it boils and becomes very thick. Then pour it into dishes. When cold, turn it into plates and eat it with what you please, either wine and sugar, or milk. It eats very pretty with cyder and sugar.

You may observe to put a great deal of water to the oatmeal, and when you pour off the last water, pour on just enough fresh to strain the oatmeal well. Some let it stand forty eight hours, some three days, shifting the water every twelve hours; but that is as you like it for sweetness or tartness. Groats once cut, does better than oatmeal. Mind to stir it together when you put in fresh water.

Butter mold.

Chap. XV

Of Jellies, Giams, and Custards

Calf's Feet Jelly

Cut four calf's feet in pieces, put them into a pipkin, with a gallon of water, cover them close, and boil them softly till almost half be consumed, run the liquor through a sieve, and let it stand till it be cold. Then with a knife take off the fat, at top and bottom, and melt the fine part of the jelly in a preserving pan or skillet, and put in a pint of Rhenish wine, the juice of four or five lemons, double refined sugar to your taste, the whites of eight eggs beaten to a froth; stir and boil all these together near half an hour; then strain it through a sieve into a jelly bag; put into your jelly-bag a very small sprig of rosemary, and a piece of lemon-peel; pass it through the bag till it is as clear as water.

Hart's-Horn Jelly

Take a large gallipot with hart's-horn; then fill it full with spring water, tie a double paper over the gallipot, and set it in a baker's oven with household bread. In the morning take it out; run it through a jelly bag; season with juice of lemons, double refined sugar, and the white of eight eggs well beaten. Let it have a boil, and run it through the jelly bag again into jelly glasses; put a bit of lemon peel in the bag.

Currant Jelly

Having stript the currants from the stalks, put them into a stone jar: STOP it close; set it in a kettle of boiling water half way up the jar; let it boil half an hour; take it out, and strain the juice through a coarse hair-sieve. To a pint of juice put a pound of sugar, set it over a fine quick clear fire in a preserving-pan or bell-metal skillet. Keep stirring it all the time till the sugar be melted; then skim the scum off as fast as it rises.

When the jelly is very clear and fine, pour it into earthen or china cups or galli-pots. When cold, cut white paper, just the bigness of the top of the pot, and lay on the jelly; dip those papers in brandy; then cover the top close with white paper, and prick it full of holes. Set it in a dry place. You may put some into glasses, for present use.

Rasberry Giam

Take a pint of currant jelly, and a quart of rasberries, bruise them well together, set them over a slow fire, keeping it stirring all the time till it boils. Let it boil five or six minutes, pour it into gallipots, paper them as you do currant jelly, and keep it for use. They will keep for two or three years, and have the full flavor of the rasberry.

A Custard

Sweeten a quart of new milk to your taste; grate in a little nutmeg, beat up eight eggs well (leaving out half the whites) stir them into the milk, and bake them in china cups, or put them in a deep china dish. Have a kettle of water boiling, set the cups in, let the water come above half way, but do not let it boil too fast for fear of its getting into the cups. You may add a little rose-water and French brandy.

Boiled Custards

Put into a pint of cream two ounces of almonds, blanched and beaten very fine, with rose or orange-flower water, or a little mace; let them boil till the cream is a little thickened, then sweeten it and stir in the eggs, and keep it stirring over the fire, till it is as thick as you would have it; then put to it a little orange-flower water, stir it well together, and put it into china cups.

N.B. You may make them without almonds.

Almond Custards

Take a pint of cream, blanch and beat a quarter of a pound of almonds fine, with two spoonfuls of rose-water. Sweeten it to your palate. Beat up the yolks of four eggs, stir all together one way over the fire, till it is thick; then pour it out into cups. Or you may bake it in little china cups.

Rice Custard

Boil a quart of cream with a blade of mace, and a quartered nutmeg, put thereto boiled rice, well beaten with the cream; mix them together, stirring them all the while they boil. When enough take it off, and sweeten it to your taste; put in a little orange flower water, then pour it into dishes. When cold, serve it.

A dairy oar was used to stir the milk and cheese.

Chap. XVI

Potting and Collaring

Of Potting

To Pot Beef or Venison

When you have boiled or baked, and cut your meat small, let it be well beaten in a marble mortar, with some butter melted for that purpose, and two or three anchovies, till you find it mellow, and agreeable to your palate. Then put it close down in pots, and pour over them a sufficient quantity of clarified butter. You may season your ingredients with what spice you please.

To Pot Pigeons or Any Other Fowls

Your pigeons being trussed and seasoned with savory spice, put them in a pot, cover them with butter, and bake them; then take them out and drain them, and when they are cold cover them with clarified butter. The same way you may pot fish, only bone them when they are baked.

To Pot Charrs or Trout

Clean the fish well and bone them; wash them with vinegar, cut off the tails, fins, and heads; then season them with pepper, salt, nutmeg, and a few cloves; then put them close in a pot, bake them with a little verjuice and some butter; then pour off the liquor, and cover them with clarified butter.

To Pot Lampreys or Eels

Take lampreys or eels, skin, gut, and wash them and slit them down the back; take out the bones, and cut them in pieces to fit your pot; then season them with pepper, salt, and nutmeg, and put them in the pot, with half a pint of vinegar. They must be close covered, and bake half an hour; and when done, pour off the liquor, and cover them with clarified butter.

Of Collaring

How to Collar Beef

Lay a flank of beef in ham-brine a fortnight; then take it out and dry it in a cloth; lay it on a board, take out all the leather and skin, cut it cross and cross; season it with savoury spice, two anchovies, and a handful or two of thyme, parsley, sweet marjoram, winter savory, onions, and fennell; strew it on the meat, roll it in a hard collar in a cloth, sew it close, tie it at both ends, and put it in a collar pot with a pint of claret, cochineal, and two quarts of pump water. When it is cold, take it out of the cloth.

White-tailed deer.

To Collar a Breast of Veal

Bone the veal, season it all over the inside with cloves, mace, and salt beat fine, a handful of sweet-herbs stripped of the stalks, and a little sage, penny-royal and parsley shred very fine, then roll it up as you do brawn; bind it with narrow tape very close, then tie a cloth round it, and boil it very tender in vinegar and water, a like quantity, with a little cloves, mace, pepper and salt, all whole. Make it boil, then put in the collars, when boiled tender, take them up, and when both are cold, take off the cloth, lay the collar in an earthen pan, and pour the liquor over; cover it close, and keep it for use.

To Collar a Breast of Mutton

Cut off the red skin, and take out the bones and gristles. Then take grated white bread, a little cloves, mace, salt and pepper, the yolks of three hard eggs bruised small, and a little lemon peel shred fine; with which, having laid the meat even and flat, season it all over, and add four or five anchovies washed and boned: then roll the meet like a collar, and bind it with coarse tape, and bake, boil, or roast it.

To Collar Pork

Bone a breast of pork, season it with savory seasoning, a good quantity of thyme, parsley and sage; then roll it in a hard collar in a cloth, tie it at both ends and boil it; and when it is cold, steep it in the savoury liquor, in which it was boiled.

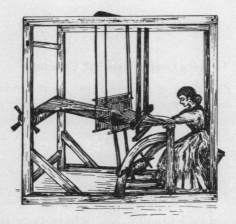

The big looms were made by carpenters, wedged together rather than nailed, so that they could be taken apart when not in use. Each part of the loom had to be exactly square that it might weave a straight web.

To Collar Eels

Scour large silver eels with salt, slit them down the back, take out all the bones; then wash and dry them, and season them with savoury spice, minced parsley, thyme, sage, and onion; and roll each in little collars in a cloth, and tie them close. Then boil them in water and salt, with the heads and bones, half a pint of vinegar, a faggot of herbs, some ginger, and a pennyworth of isinglass; when they are tender, take them up, tie them close again, strain the pickle and keep the eels in it.

Chap. XVII

Of Preserving, Drying, and Candying

To Keep Green Pease Till Christmas

Take fine young pease, shell them, throw them into a cullender to drain, then lay a cloth four or five times double on a table, and spread them on; dry them very well, and have your bottles ready, fill them and cover them with mutton suet fat; when it is a little cool, fill the necks almost to the top, cork them, tie a bladder and a lath over them, and set them in a cool dry place.

To Keep French Beans All the Year

Take young beans gathered on a dry day, have a large stone jar ready, lay a layer of salt at the bottom, and a layer of beans, then salt, and then beans, and so on till the jar is full; cover them with salt, and tie a coarse cloth over them and a board on that, and then a weight to keep it close from all air; set them in a dry cellar and when you use them, take some out and cover them close again; wash them you took out very clean, and let them lie in soft water twenty-four hours, shifting the water often; when you boil them do not put any salt in the water.

To Keep White Bullace, Pear, Plumbs, or Damsons, &c for Tarts or Pies

Gather them when full grown, and just as they begin to turn. Pick all the largest out, save about two thirds of the fruit, to the other third put as much water as you think will cover them, boil and skim them; when the fruit is boiled very soft, strain it through a course hair-sieve; and to every quart of this liquor put a pound and a half of sugar, boil it, and skim it very well; then throw in your fruit, just give them a scald; take them off the fire, and when cold, put them into bottles with wide mouths, pour your syrup over them, lay a piece of white paper over them, and cover them with oil.

To Make Marmalade

To two pounds of quinces put three quarters of a pound of sugar and a pint of spring-water, then put them over the fire, and boil them until they are tender; then take them up and bruise them; then put them into the liquor, let it boil three quarters of an hour, and then put it into your pots or saucers.

To Preserve Mulberries Whole

Set some mulberries over the fire in a skillet or preserving pan; draw from them a pint of juice when it is strained; then take three pounds of sugar beaten very fine, wet the sugar with the pint of juice, boil up your sugar and skim it, put in two pounds of ripe mulberries, and let them stand in the syrup till they are thoroughly warm, then set them on the fire, and let them boil very gently; do them but half enough, so put them by in the syrup till next day, then boil them gently again: when the syrup is pretty thick, and will stand in round drops when it is cold, they are enough, so put all into a gallipot for use.

To Preserve Gooseberries, Damsons, or Plumbs

Gather them when dry, full grown, and not ripe; pick them one by one, put them into glass bottles that are very clean and dry, and cork them close with new corks; then put a kettle of water on the fire, and put in the bottles with care; wet not the corks, but let the water come up to the necks; make a gentle fire till they are a little coddled and turn white; do not take them up till cold, then pitch the corks all over, or wax them close and thick; then set them in a cool dry cellar.

To Preserve Peaches

Put your peaches in boiling water, just give them a scald; but don't let them boil, take them out, and put them in cold water, then dry them in a sieve, and put them in long, wide-mouthed bottles; to half a dozen peaches take a quarter of a pound of sugar clarify it, pour it over your peaches, and fill the bottles with brandy. Stop them close and keep them in a close place.

To Preserve Apricots

Take your apricots and pare them, then save what you can whole; give them a light boiling in a pint of water, according to your quantity of fruit; then take the weight of your apricots in sugar, and take the liquor which you boil them in, and your sugar, and boil it till it comes to a syrup, and give them a light boiling taking off the scum as it rises. When the syrup jellies it is enough; then take up the apricots, and cover them with the jelly and put cut paper over them, and lay them down when cold.

To Preserve Apricots Green

Take apricots when they are young and tender, coddle them a little, rub them with a coarse cloth to take off the skin, and throw them into water as you do them, and put them in the same water they were coddled in; cover them with vine leaves, a white paper, or something more at the top; the closer you keep them, the sooner they are green: be sure you don't let them boil; when they are green weigh them and to every pound of apricots, take a pound of loaf sugar, put it into a pan, and to every pound of sugar a gill of water, boil your sugar and water a little, and scum it, then put in your apricots; let them boil together till your fruit looks clear & your syrup thick, skim it all the time it is boiling, and put them into a pot covered with paper dipped in brandy.

Or,

Take your plumbs before they have stones in them, which you may know by putting a pin through them, then coddle them in many waters, till they are as green as grass: peel them and coddle them again; you must take the weight of them in sugar and make a syrup; put to your sugar a pint of water; then put them in, set them on the fire to boil slowly, till they be clear, skimming them often, and they will be very green. Put them up in glasses, and keep them for use.

To Preserve Cherries

Take two pounds of cherries, one pound and a half of sugar, half a pint of fair water, melt your sugar in it; when it is melted, put in your other sugar and your cherries; then boil them softly, till all the sugar be melted; then boil them fast, and skim them; take them off two or three times and shake them, and put them on again, and let them boil fast; and when they are of a good colour, and the syrup will stand, they are enough.

To Preserve Rasberries

Chuse rasberries that are not too ripe, and take the weight of them in sugar, wet your sugar with a little water, and put in your berries, and let them boil softly; take heed of breaking them; when they are clear, then take them up, and boil the syrup till it be thick enough, then put them in again; and when they are cold, put them up in glasses.

To Preserve Currants

Take the weight of the currants in sugar, pick out the seeds; take to a pound of sugar, half a pint of water; let it melt; then put in your berries, and let them do very leisurely, skim them, and take them up, let the syrup boil; then put them on again; and when they are clear, and the syrup thick enough, take them off; and when they are cold, put them up in glasses.

To Dry Peaches

Take the fairest and ripest peaches, pare them into fair water; take their weight in double refined sugar: of one half make a very thin syrup; then put in your peaches, boiling them till they look clear; then split and stone them. Boil them till they are very tender, lay them a-draining, take the other half of the sugar, and boil it almost to a candy; then put in your peaches, and let them lie all night, then lay them on a glass, and set them in a stove, till they are dry. If they are sugar'd too much, wipe them with a wet cloth a little: Let the first syrup be very thin, a quart of water to a pound of sugar.

To Dry Cherries

To four pounds of cherries, put one pound of sugar, and just put as much water to the sugar as will wet it; when it is melted, make it boil, stone your cherries, put them in, and make them boil; skim them two or three times, take them off, and let them stand in the syrup two or three days, then boil your syrup and put it to them again, but don't boil your cherries any more. Let them stand three or four days longer, then take them out, lay them in sieves to dry when dry lay them in rows on papers, and do a row of cherries, and a row of white paper in boxes.

To Candy Angelica

Take it in *April,* boil it in water till it be tender, then take it up and drain it from the water very well; then scrape the outside of it, and dry it in a clean cloth, and lay it in the syrup, and let it lie in three or four days, and cover it close: the syrup must be strong of sugar, and keep it hot a good while, but let it not boil; after it is heated a good while, lay it upon a pie plate, and so let it dry; keep it near the fire, lest it dissolve.

Chap. XVIII

Of Pickling

To Pickle Asparagus

Gather your asparagus, and lay them in an earthen pot; make a brine of water and salt strong enough to bear an egg, pour it hot on them, and keep it close covered. When you use them hot, lay them in cold water two hours, then boil and butter them for table. If you can use them as a pickle, boil them and lay them in vinegar.

To Pickle Nasturtium Buds or Seeds

Take the seeds new off the plant when they are pretty large, but before they grow hard, and throw them into the best white wine vinegar that has been boiled up with what spice you please. Keep them close stopped in a bottle. They are fit for use in eight days.

To Pickle or Make Mangos of Melons

Take green Melons, as many as you please, and make a brine strong enough to bear an egg; then pour it boiling hot on the melons, keeping them down under the brine; let them stand five or six days; then take them out, slit them down on one side, take out all the seeds, scrape them well on the inside, and wash them clean with cold water; then take a clove of garlick, a little ginger and nutmeg sliced, and a little whole pepper; put all these proportionably into the melons, filling them up with mustard-seeds; then lay them in an earthen pot with the split upwards, and take one part of mustard and two parts of vinegar, enough to cover them, pouring it upon them scalding hot, and keep them close stopped.

To Pickle Mushrooms White

Cut the stem of your small buttons at the bottom; wash them in two or three waters with a piece of flannel. Have in readiness a stew-pan on the fire, with some spring water that has had a handful of common salt thrown into it; and as soon as it boils, put in your buttons. When they have boiled about three or four minutes, take them off the fire, and throw them into a cullender; from thence spred them as quick as you can upon a linen cloth, & cover them with another. Have ready several wide mouth bottles; and as you put in the mushrooms, now and then mix a blade or two of mace, and some nutmeg sliced amongst them; then fill your bottle with distilled vinegar. If you pour over them some melted mutton fat, that has been well strained, it will keep them better than oil itself would.

To Pickle Barberries

Take of white wine vinegar and water of each an equal quantity: to every quart of this liquor, put in half a pound of sixpenny sugar, then pick the worst of your barberries and put them into this liquor, and the best into glasses; then boil your pickle with the worst of your barberries, and skim it very clean. Boil it till it looks of a fine colour, then let it stand to be cold, before you strain it; then strain it through a cloth, wringing it to get all the colour you can from the barberries. Let it stand to cool and settle, then pour it clear into the glasses. In a little of the pickle boil a little fennel; when cold, put a little bit at the top of the pot or glass, and cover it close with a bladder and leather. To every half pound of sugar, put a quarter of a pound of white salt.

To Pickle Radish-Pods

Make a strong pickle, with cold spring-water and bay salt, strong enough to bear an egg, then put your pods in, and lay a thin board on them, to keep them under water. Let them stand ten days, then drain them in a sieve, and lay them on a cloth to dry; then take white wine vinegar, as much as you think will cover them, boil it, and put your pods in a jar, with ginger, mace, cloves, Jamaica pepper. Pour your vinegar boiling hot on, cover them with a coarse cloth, three or four times double, that the steam may come through a little, and let them stand two days. Repeat this two or three times; when it is cold put in a pint of mustard seed, and some horse-radish; cover it close.

To Pickle Samphire

Lay what quantity you think proper of such samphire as is green in a clean pan, and (after you have thrown two or three handfuls of salt over it) cover it with spring water. When it has lain for four and twenty hours, put it into a brass sauce-pan, that has been well cleaned; and when you have thrown into it one handful only of salt, cover it with the best vinegar. Cover your sauce-pan close, and set it over a gentle fire; let it stand no longer than till it is just crisp and green, for it would be utterly spoiled should it stand till it be soft. As soon as you have taken it off the fire, pour it into your pickling pot, and take care to cover it close.

To Pickle Onions

Take small onions, lay them in salt and water a day, and shift them in that time once; then dry them in a cloth, and take some white wine vinegar, cloves, mace, and a little pepper; boil this pickle and pour over them, and when it is cold, cover them close.

Or,

Take small white onions, lay them in water and salt, and put to them a pickle of vinegar and spice.

To Pickle Cabbage

Take a large fine cabbage, and cut it in thin slices, season some vinegar with what spice you think fit, then pour it on scalding hot, two or three times.

To Pickle French Beans

Gather them before they have strings, and put them into a very strong brine of water and salt for nine days; then drain them from the brine; and put boiling hot vinegar to them, and stop them close twenty four hours; do so for four or five days following, and they will turn green; then put to a peck of beans half an ounce of cloves and mace, as much pepper, a handful of dill and fennel, and two or three bay leaves. You may do broom buds, and purslane stalks the same way, only let them lie twenty four hours, and no longer; if they do not turn green, you set them on the fire in the pickle, and let them stand close covered and just warm them; for if they boil, they are spoiled.

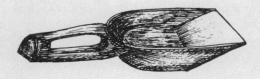

To Pickle Cucumbers

Let your cucumbers be small, fresh gathered, and free from spots; then make a pickle of salt and water, strong enough to bear an egg; boil the pickle and skim it well, and then pour it upon your cucumbers, and stive them down for twenty four hours; then strain them out into a cullender, and dry them well with a cloth, and take the best white wine vinegar, with cloves, sliced mace, nutmeg, white pepper corns, long pepper and races of ginger, (as much as you please) boil them up together, and then clap the cucumbers in, with a few vine leaves, and a little salt, and as soon as they begin to turn their colour, put them into jars, stive them down close, and when cold, tie on a bladder and leather.

Chap. XIX

Of Made Wines

To Make Gooseberry Wine

Take gooseberries when they are just beginning to turn ripe, bruise them well, but not so as to break their stones, pour to every eight pounds of pulp a gallon of spring water, and let them stand in the vessel covered, in a cool place, twenty-four hours; then put them into a strong canvas or hair bag, and press out all the juice that will run from them, and to every quart of it put twelve ounces of loaf sugar, stirring it about till it be melted; then put it up into a well seasoned cask, and set it in a cool place; when it has purged and settled about twenty or thirty days, fill the vessel full, and bung it down close.

When it is well worked and settled, draw it off into bottles, and keep them in a cool place.

To Make Currant Wine

Gather your currants, when the weather is dry, and they are full ripe, strip them carefully from the stalks; put them into a pan, and bruise them with a wooden pestle; then let it stand about twenty four hours, after which strain it through a sieve. Add three pounds of fine powder sugar to every four quarts of the liquor; and then shaking or stirring it well, fill your vessel, and put about a quart of brandy to every seven gallons: As soon as it is fine, bottle it off.

To Make Raisin Wine

Put two hundred weight of raisins, with the stalks, into a hogshead, and fill it almost full with spring water; let them steep about twelve days, frequently stirring them about, and after pouring the juice off, press the raisins. Put all the liquor together in a very clean vessel. You will find it hiss for some time, and when the noise ceases, it must be stopped close, and stand for six or seven months; and when it proves fine and clear, rack it off into another vessel; stop it up, and let it remain twelve or fourteen weeks longer; then bottle it off.

To Make Rasberry Wine

Take red rasberries when they are nearly ripe; clear the husks and stalks from them, soak them in fair water, that has been boiled and sweetened with loaf sugar, a pound and a half to a gallon; when they have soaked about twelve hours, take them out, put them into a fine linen pressing bag, press out the juice into the water, then boil them up together, and scum them well twice or thrice over a gentle fire; take off the vessel, and let the liquor cool, and when the scum arises take off all that you can, and pour off the liquor into a well seasoned cask, or earthen vessel; then boil an ounce of mace, in a pint of white wine, till the third part be consumed; strain it, and add it to the liquor; when it has well settled and fermented, draw it off into a cask, or bottles, and keep it in a cool place.

Products of the cooper: tub, pipkin, barrel, and bucket.

To Make Morella Wine

Take two gallons of white wine, and twenty pounds of Morella cherries; take away the stalks, and so bruise them that the stones may be broken; press the juice into the wine; and add of mace, cinnomon, and nutmeg, an ounce of each, tied in a bag grosly bruised, and hang it in the wine when you have put it up in a cask.

To Make Elder Wine

When the elder-berries are ripe, pick them, and put them into a stone jar; set them in boiling water, or in a slack oven, 'till the jar is as warm as you can well bear to touch it with your hand; then strain the fruit through a coarse cloth, squeezing them hard, and pour the liquor into a kettle. Put it on the fire, and let it boil, and to every quart of liquor add a pound of Lisbon sugar, and scum it often. Then let it settle, and pour it off into a jar, and cover it close.

To Make Cowslip Wine

Take five pounds of loaf-sugar, and four gallons of water, simmer them half an hour, and disolve the sugar; when it is cold, put to half a peck of cowslip flowers, picked and gently bruised; then add two spoonfuls of yeast, and beat it up with a pint of syrup of lemon, and a lemon-peel or two. Pour the whole into a cask, let them stand close stopped for three days, that they may ferment; then put in some juice of cowslips, and give it room to work; when it has stood a month draw it off into bottles, putting a little lump of loaf sugar into each.

To Make Mead

To thirteen gallons of water, put thirty pounds of honey, boil and scum it well, then take rosemary, thyme, bay-leaves, and sweet-briar, one handful all together, boil it an hour; put it into a tub, with a little ground malt; stir it till it is new-milk warm; strain it through a cloth, and put it into the tub again, cut a toast, and spread it over with good yeast, and put it into the tub also, and when the liquor is covered over with yeast, put it up in a barrel; then take of cloves, mace, and nut-megs, an ounce and a half; of ginger sliced, an ounce; bruise the spice, tie it up in a rag, and hang it in the vessel; stopping it up close for use.

To Make Balm Wine

Take a peck of balm leaves, put them in a tub or large pot, heat four gallons of water scalding hot, ready to boil, then pour it upon the leaves, so let it stand all night; in the morning strain them through a hair-sieve; put to every gallon of water two pounds of fine sugar, & stir it very well; take the whites of four or five eggs, beat them very well, put them into a pan, and whisk it very well before it be over hot; when the scum begins to rise take it off, and keep it skimming all the while it is boiling; let it boil three quarters of an hour, and then put it into the tub; when it is cold put a little new yeast upon it, and beat it every two hours, that it may head the better; so work it for two days, then put it into a sweet vessel, bung it up close, and when it is fine bottle it.

Noggin, trencher, and spoon.

To Make Birch Wine

Take your birch water and boil it, and clear it with whites of eggs; to every gallon of water take two pounds and a half of fine sugar; boil it three quarters of an hour, and when it is almost cold, put in a little yeast; work it two or three days, then put it into the barrel, and to every five gallons put in a quart of brandy, and half a pound of stoned raisins. Before you put up your wine burn a brimstone match in the barrel.

To Make Orange Wine

Take six gallons of water, fifteen pounds of powder sugar, and the whites of six eggs well beaten; boil them three quarters of an hour, and skim them while any scum will rise; when it is cold enough for working, put to it six ounces of syrup of citron or lemons, and six spoonfuls of yeast; beat the syrup and yeast well together, and put in the peel and juice of fifty oranges; work it two days and a night; then turn it up into a barrel, and bottle it at three or four Months old.

FINIS

A hogshead was a large wooden cask or barrel that held up to 140 gallons.

Glossary

Acate	A purchased product, one that was not made in the home.
Ambergrease	(Ambergris) A waxlike substance found floating in the sea. A secretion in the intestines of the sperm whale. Used in perfumery as a fixative and formerly in cooking.
Angelica	(*Angelica sativa*) Found native from New England to Pennsylvania. Stems are sometimes candied. The roots are used in domestic medicine as an aromatic and stimulant. A wild parsnip that is also called Masterwort.
Assence	(Essence) A highly seasoned liquid garnish to be used in cooking. Made from any well-cured pork pieces, usually ham.
Balm	(*Mellissa officinalis*) An aromatic perennial used as an herbage in seasonings and liquors. In its green state it has an odor of lemon and is used in the place of lemon thyme.
Barberry	(*Berberis canadensis*) A shrub found in the Alleghenies of Virginia and to the south. The berries are red and have a pleasantly agreeable acid taste.
Battalia pie	A pie of various tidbits such as cockscombs, sweetbreads, livers, and gizzards.
Beards	The rows of gills found in certain bivalves such as oysters.
Bell metal	A variety of bronze consisting usually of three or four parts of copper to one of tin, used for making bells and other fine metal objects.
Bladder and Leather	The membrane of a sheep's or ox's bladder used for an air-tight covering and tied with a leather thong.
Brace	Two of anything, as a brace of fowl. A pair.
Brawn	The flesh of the boar (often defined as the "brawn of the boar" as early as the sixteenth century). In recent use, the flesh of a boar or swine, collared, boiled and pickled or potted.
Bray	To beat small, to bruise, pound or crush to a powder, usually in a mortar. "Bray the hard part in a mortar."
Brimstone	Common vernacular name for sulphur.
Broad bean	A large, smooth, flattish bean, usually either a lima or a fava.
Broom buds	Small flower buds found on a shrub of the pea family.
Bullace	A small wild plum. There are two kinds, the dark bullace and the white.
Callapach	(Calipash or Carapace) The upper shell of a turtle.
Callapee	Lower shell or plastron of a turtle.
Candy	A verb used to describe the method of preserving with sugar.
Case	To strip the skin from a bird or animal.
Cat whipper	A man who both made and repaired shoes.

Caudle
A warm drink that was given to sick persons.
A mixture of wine or ale with eggs, bread or gruel, seasoned with sugar and spices.

Chandler
Candlemaker.

Charr
A fish of the trout family.

Chine
The backbone or spine. Chine is the two loins taken together in mutton, the "saddle" in beef.

Chump
The thick, blunt end of the loin.

Cochineal
A dye or food coloring made from the dried bodies of females of a scale insect. It may also refer to the bright red of some grains or berries.

Coddle
To cook slowly and gently.

Coddlin
(Codlin) A small, immature apple.

Coffin
A mold of paste for a pie.

Collared
Rolled in a cloth and fastened. The cloth is sometimes sewed around the meat or fish to keep it fastened tight. The ends are tied.

Collops
Small pieces or slices of meat.

Comfits
A small treat of fruit or some other tidbit preserved with sugar, as a candy covered almond or a sugarplum.

Cooper
The man who made barrels and other containers with staved sides and hoops to hold them together.

Cordwainer
Shoemaker.

Cullis
A strong, clear broth, as a beef tea. A meat jelly.

Dresser
A sideboard or table in a kitchen on which food was prepared.

Dutch oven
A cast-iron pot with a heavy lid that has an upright rim. The lid can be covered with coals from the fire, thus cooking from both top and bottom.

Ell rule
A measuring device generally used to measure cloth. An ell rule was forty-five inches long.

Eringo
(Eryngo) (*Eryngium maritimum*) Sea eryngo, sea holly or sea holm. The tender young shoots are blanched and eaten like asparagus. The roots are candied and when boiled or roasted are similar to chestnuts.

Faggot
A bundle or a bunch, as a "faggot of herbs."

Fireback
A sheet of iron, sometimes with a design, used in the back of a fireplace to reflect the heat out into the room.

Flummery
A kind of food made from wheat flour or oatmeal. A name given to various sweet dishes that were made with milk, flour, eggs and spices.

Forcemeat
Meat that has been chopped fine and highly seasoned for use as a stuffing or garnish.

Froth
Meat basted with butter while still turning on the spit and then dusted lightly with flour will form a froth or bubbling effect on the surface.

Gallipot
A small earthen pot that is glazed.

Giblets
The portions that are taken out or cut off before cooking. The liver and gizzard, etc., as well as the pinions and feet.

Gill	One-fourth pint, U.S. measure. An old English measure equal to one-half pint.
Gobbets	Small pieces or portions of meat.
Griskin	A pork loin or especially the lean part.
Groats	Hulled or hulled and broken grain of various kinds. Usually oats, but may also include wheat, barley, or maize.
Gudgeons	Small fish also known as goby or rockfish.
Hair sieve	A strainer made with a haircloth bottom.
Haircloth	A stiff, wiry fabric with a hair weft (camel's hair or horsehair) and a cotton or linen warp.
Harshed	Hashed, cut small.
Hartshorn jelly	A nutritive jelly made formerly by shaving the hart's (deer's) horns. Now made from the bones of calves.
Hoop	A circular tin mold or pan used to contain the batter while baking.
Horns	Pointed and tapered skewers.
Isinglass	A very pure form of gelatin prepared from the air bladders of sturgeons or other fish. Used in making jellies.
Lambstones	The testicles of sheep used as a food.
Lear	A thick sauce or gravy, or the thickening for such a sauce.
Lights	The lungs of animals, used as food.
Linsey-woolsey	A very sturdy fabric made with a linen warp and a woolen filling.
Lisbon sugar	A soft sugar as opposed to the hard lump or loaf form that was most common.
Lumber pie	(Lombard pie?) A pie in which balls of minced meat or fish are baked with butter and eggs.
Mace	External covering of the nutmeg.
Maids	A name used for certain fish, as the skate or thornback, when they are young.
Mallows	Originally a potherb native to Europe and Asia, it arrived in America before 1669 and is now naturalized. A culinary herb similar to spinach.
Manchet	A small roll or loaf of the finest wheaten bread, round and flattish, thicker in the middle than at the ends.
Marrow pudding	A pudding made with the marrow or fatty substance from inside the larger bones of animals. A buttery shortening used in cooking.
Middlings	When flour was ground at home it was carefully sifted and separated. This would be neither the coarsest nor the finest flour.
Moralla	(Morello) Any of several cherries with red skin and flesh and having a pleasantly high acidity.
Morels	An edible fungus, a mushroom. Native in most of the eastern United States.
Musk	A substance obtained from a sac about the size of an egg found under the skin on the abdomen of the male musk deer. Used as a basis for perfumes.
Neat's tongue	The tongue of an ox, bullock, cow, or heifer.

Niddy-noddy	(Niddle-noddle) To nod rapidly to and fro, hence a name given to a device used to wind and measure yarn.
Ortolans	Small, buntinglike birds.
Pack thread	Heavy thread or twine.
Palates	The bone and flesh structure of the roof of the mouth.
Pap sauce	Bread boiled or softened in milk or water. A bread sauce.
Peck	A measure of capacity used for dry goods. One-fourth part of a bushel or two gallons.
Peel	A long-handled, shovel-like tool used to put bread into or remove from the baker's oven.
Pennyroyal	A perennial mint.
Pettitoes	The feet of a pig, especially when used as a food. Pig's trotters is another name. Before 1600 it seems to have included the heart, liver, lungs, etc., not only of the pig, but also calves, sheep, and other animals.
Pipkin	A small cask or vessel with staved sides, with one stave longer than the others which served as a handle of sorts.
Plaice	Generally a flounder or other flat fish.
Plovers	(*Charadriidae*) Common name for several small birds including snipes and sandpipers.
Pluck	The heart, liver, and lungs used as a food.
Portable soup	"Soup-in-your-pocket." Meat was cooked until it was reduced to a gluelike substance and then dried. By adding water at a later time it could be converted back into a broth.
Prunellas	(*Prunella vulgaris*) A common weed also known as "self-heal."
Pudding	A mixture of meat, suet, and seasonings thickened with flour or meal and enclosed in an animal stomach to be cooked. A sort of sausage.
Purslane	An herb from the *Portulacaceae* family. The fleshy, succulent leaves were used as a vegetable.
Roes	The strips of eggs found in the female fish just before the time of spawning.
Quartern loaf	Quartern by itself means one fourth. As bakers were required to make loaves that weighed a full pound, the quartern loaf designated a loaf of bread weighing one quarter of a pound.
Quick	Alive. Used in combination with other words, as the "quick and the dead." A "quick hedge" was used in Europe as a fence. Wood was so plentiful in this country that fencing with rails and logs became an American art form.
Quick oven	A hot oven. Testing of an oven was done by throwing in some white flour. A slow oven would turn it to a straw color in five minutes, a medium one to a light brown, and a hot (quick) oven to a dark brown.
Raced	Shredded, cut, or slashed.
Rasher	A thin slice of bacon or ham cooked (or intended to be cooked) by boiling or frying.
Rasped	(Also raspings) Grated, as "bread raspings."
Ratafia cakes	Small sweet cakes or biscuits made with almond paste.

Rennet	(Also runnet) A mass of curdled milk found in the stomach of an unweaned calf. It was used for curdling milk in the making of cheese. Also a preparation of the inner membrane of the stomach used for this and other purposes. To curdle milk with rennet.
Roach	A small fresh-water fish of the carp family.
Ruffs and Reefs	(Reeves) These are small birds of the sandpiper family. Ruff is the male, reeve the female.
Sack	Generally a sherry wine, but sometimes used for any white wine.
Samphire	(*Echinophora spinosa*) The prickly sea parsnip. The fleshy leaves were used as pickles.
Savoy biscuit	A kind of sponge biscuit made of finger-shaped pieces of paste, joined together in pairs.
Savoy cake	A large sponge cake baked in a mold.
Savoys	A rough-leafed variety of the common cabbage grown for winter use.
Scate	Also skate. (*Raia*) The common species, *Raia batis* is very large, flat, cartilaginous fish much used as food.
Scotch	To cut shallow diagonal slashes in the skin.
Scrag	The lean and inferior end of a neck of mutton or veal.
Shivered	Broken into pieces. Shivered palates would refer to the bone and flesh structure of the roof of an animal's mouth broken up for cooking.
Sippet	A small piece of dried or toasted bread, frequently cut into triangles, usually served in soup or broth. They might also be served with a meat dish and used for dipping into the gravy. A small sop.
Slice	A spatulalike utensil used for mixing or stirring. One of several flattish utensils, usually perforated, used for various purposes in cookery. A fish slice was used to lift the cooked fish from the broth without breaking the pieces.
Soals	(Soles) (*Solea*) A common flat fish highly esteemed as a food.
Soleratus	(Saleratus) An impure bicarbonate of potash containing more carbon dioxide than pearl ash does, much used as an ingredient in baking powders.
Sorrel	(*Rumex*) Any of certain small perennial plants. Characterized by a sour taste and cultivated for culinary purposes or medicine.
Sounds	Swimming bladders of certain fish, especially of a cod or sturgeon.
Soup meagre	(Soup maigre) A thin soup made from vegetables or fish.
Souse	Prepare or preserve for food by pickling. Also the liquid in which the pickling process is done.
Spile	A hollow wooden pipe that is tapped into a maple tree to let out the sap which is then boiled to a syrup or sugar.
Spitchcocked	A method of preparing an eel. The eel is cut into short pieces, dipped in bread crumbs and chopped herbs and then broiled or fried.

Stive	To compress or pack tightly. To crowd together.
Stove	A boiling pot designed with a tight fitting cover in which to "stove" or "sweat" meat or game. A "stoving pot."
Sweetbreads	The pancreas or the thymus gland of an animal used as a food. Considered a delicacy.
Syllabub	(Sillabub) A drink or a dish made from cream or milk (frequently warm from the cow), curdled by adding wine, cider, or other acid and usually sweetened or flavored.
Tammy	Cloth made from wool or a wool and cotton combination. A strainer or sieve made from this material was also a "tammy."
Tench	(*Tinca vulgaris*) A thick-bodied fresh-water fish similar to the carp.
Thornback	(*Raia clavata*) A flat fish, as a ray or skate, having several rows of short, sharp spines along the back and tail.
Trade signs	Almost every shop had a carved wooden sign to show the type of business conducted within.
Trail	The liquor which runs from cooking meat.
Treenware	Old name given to wooden utensils made by hand with primitive tools. Treen was the plural form for tree.
Trencher	A flat piece of wood, round or square, on which meat was served and cut. A wooden plate or platter.
Trotters	The feet of sheep or pigs used as a food.
Truffle	Any one of several edible fungi that grow underground. A great delicacy varying in size from a walnut to a large potato.
Truss	To bind, tie, or fasten the wings and legs of a fowl or the legs of an animal to the body with skewers or string in preparing it for cooking.
Udder	A pendulous bag in which milk is held in certain female animals.
Umble Pie	Umbles were the edible inward parts, heart, liver, and entrails, usually of a deer. The high-ranking members of a family or guests dined on venison while lower members of the household ate pie made from umbles. Origin of the expression to "eat humble pie" meaning to lower one's self or to defer to others.
Verjuice	An acid juice of green or unripe grapes, crabapples, or other sour fruit, squeezed and made into a liquor. Used in cooking.
Wallops	The series of noisy bubbling motions made by water reaching the boiling point, or boiling rapidly. One of such bubbling motions used as a vague measure of time in cooking.
Whey	The serum, or watery part of milk that is left after the removal of the curd.
Wigeons	(Widgeons) A wild duck.
Wigs	A cake or a bun flavored with spices and caraway seeds, and frequently calling for dried currants.